RESEARCH HIGHLIGHTS
IN SOCIAL WORK

12 — The Family: Context or Client?

RESEARCH HIGHLIGHTS IN SOCIAL WORK

12 — THE FAMILY: CONTEXT OR CLIENT?

Kogan Page

University of Aberdeen
Department of Social Work
King's College
Aberdeen

First published in 1986 by Kogan Page Ltd
120 Pentonville Road, London N1 9JN

British Library Cataloguing in Publication Data
The Family: context or client? – (Research highlights in social work; 12)
1. Problem families – Great Britain
2. Family social work – Great Britain
1. Title II. Series
326.8′28′0941 HV700.G7

ISBN 1-85091-025-1 (hb)
ISBN 1-85091-026-X (pb)

Printed in Great Britain by
Biddles Ltd, Guildford

LIST OF CONTENTS

Contributors

Gordon Horobin	Taught Sociology at Hull University before joining the MRC Medical Sociology Unit at Aberdeen where he was Assistant Director. He now holds appointments in the Departments of Social Work and of Sociology at Aberdeen and is continuing to carry out research on aspects of General Practice.
Christopher Turner	Professor of Sociology at the University of Stirling. He has a longstanding research interest in the comparative study of kinship and domestic organisation, and in the organisation of health and social services. He has recently completed a pilot study of programmes concerned with the transition of young people from residential care to independent living, and is currently working on a much broader comparative study of child-care policies and practices in Sweden and Scotland.
David Lessels	Lecturer in family law at Aberdeen University, with particular interests in the law on child-care and mental health, and family conciliation services. Teaches law to students taking the Certificate in Applied Social Studies, and has been involved recently in training mental health officers. He is a former member of the adoption committee of Voluntary Services Aberdeen.
Malcolm Wicks	Director of the independent Family Policy Studies Centre, and was previously the Research Director and Secretary of the Study Commission on the Family. Formerly he was a lecturer at Brunel University and the Civil Service College, and he has also worked in the Home Office. He has written extensively on social policy issues. His publications include: *Old and Cold: Hypothermia and Social Policy* (Heinemann, 1978) and *Government and Urban Poverty* (Basil Blackwell, 1983) of which he was co-author.
Marion Lowe	Marion Lowe worked as a social worker in London and the USA, as a Women's Rights Officer and as a Lecturer in Social Policy and Social Work. She is currently Assistant Director (Training and Development) of a Social Services Department.

Laurence Tasker	Head of the Department of Administration and Social Studies at Teesside Polytechnic. He has formerly lectured in Sociology and Social Policy at the Universities of Birmingham, Wales and Surrey.
David Gough	Research Psychologist at the Social Paediatric and Obstetric Research Unit, University of Glasgow. He is at present completing a study of family change and agency decision making in child abuse. This is being followed by a literature and practice review of intervention strategies that have been used in these cases. The studies are on behalf of SWSG, Scottish Office, and DHSS respectively.
Andrew Boddy	Director of the Social Paediatric and Obstetric Research Unit, University of Glasgow. He is a community physician and is involved in a wide range of studies concerned with child health that are being undertaken in the Unit.
Hugh Jenkins	Senior Social Worker and Family Therapist in the Department of Children and Adolescents, Maudsley Hospital, London. He is also Hon. Senior Clinical Tutor at the Institute of Psychiatry, London, a Member of the Institute of Family Therapy, and was Chairman of the Association for Family Therapy from 1982 to 1985.
Douglas Chisholm	Douglas Chisholm trained in medicine at Aberdeen University, in general psychiatry at the Royal Cornhill Hospital and the Ross Clinic, Aberdeen, and in child and family psychiatry at the Royal Aberdeen Children's Hospital. He has also studied at the Clark Institute of Psychology in Toronto. Since 1975, he has been Consultant in Child and Adolescent Psychiatry at the Department of Child and Family Psychiatry, Royal Aberdeen Children's Hospital, and Clinical Senior Lecturer at the University of Aberdeen. His interests lie in play and other forms of psychotherapy with children and adolescents and in family therapy.
Linda Hunt	Linda Hunt completed her social work training at the University of Edinburgh. She worked as a practitioner in a variety of settings in Scotland and England before

becoming Lecturer in Social Work at the University of Manchester. She returned to Edinburgh to join the Central Advisory Service of Social Work Services Group in 1978 where her particular interests are methods of intervention and the organisation of social work services. She continues to practise as a volunteer counsellor in alcoholism and for three years has been co-director of a series of workshops and conferences on the management of helping relationships in India.

EDITORIAL

Gordon Horobin

Any collection of papers on social work and families will inevitably look unbalanced from some points of view. This volume is no exception. The family is so deeply involved in all aspects of our lives that it can never be ignored in any exploration of individual behaviour or interpersonal relationships, or, therefore, in any service intervention. But what *is* the family? And is the family relevant to practice only as the context within which problems arise and are addressed, or is it the family rather than the individual which is the client? These issues are clearly important in relationship to a host of problems or fields of practice not discussed here; for example, delinquency, foster care, disability, ageing and housing. Comprehensive coverage was not possible. Instead we have chosen to focus upon just a few areas, each of which will, we assume, figure in the case-loads of social service departments and of practising social workers.

The first three chapters are intended as 'background' to the five 'service' chapters which follow. Clearly the distinction is only partial. In considering the legal framework, for example, questions are raised about the appropriateness or otherwise of family courts, and an analysis of family poverty, especially by the director of the Family Policy Studies Centre, would seem odd without some discussion of policy.

In the first chapter, then, Turner examines the family as both an institution and as ideology. He shows how contemporary notions of what the family is and what it should do are shaped by historical changes and by conventional moralities. It is, of course, well known that the relative weights of consanguinity and conjugality have shown considerable variation over time and space. The modern Western family appears to contain ambiguities and tensions between the two. Traditional values emphasise the obligations of close kinship – parents to children, children to ageing parents – while the current rates of divorce and separation perhaps indicate an increasing concern with the quality of conjugal relationships. Turner points to a set of influences which have perhaps been unduly neglected in the research literature on the family, if not by contemporary moralists – the media. He suggests that, since almost every conceivable form of family and family problem is displayed on television, the medium provides a sort of supermarket of images and models which people may use as comparisons for their own experiences. He concludes that theory building in this field has lagged behind empirical description and that the relative importance of structural and cultural forces on the one hand and individual negotiations and interactions on the other, in explaining variations in family forms, remains rather obscure.

Legislation has, in the main, reinforced individual rights, especially of children, rather than the corporate rights of families. Family law has grown substantially in the past two or three decades as the consequences of divorce and remarriage for family members have become more apparent. David Lessels' paper, concentrating especially on Scots Law, sets out some of these legislative changes. While the law gives precedence to the needs of children for protection and provision for their basic well-being and, to a perhaps lesser extent, the protection of women from domestic violence, it also underwrites the essential privacy of the family. That the rights of children and of parents may often conflict is obvious and all legislation affecting the family is therefore inevitably a compromise. The growth of conciliation services reflects this and some countries have gone further in instituting Family Courts. Lessels concludes that the combination in Scotland of the sheriff court and children's hearings adequately covers the duties of a Family Court, although out of court conciliation services could usefully supplement these. There would seem to be little chance of additional public finance being made available for such an exercise, however. Voluntary agencies may fill the gap and, depending on their point of view, will regard it as opportunity or burden, or, more likely, an uneasy combination of the two.

The extent and causes of poverty are discussed in the third chapter, by Malcolm Wicks. Whether defined in absolute or relative terms, and however it is measured, poverty is now a mass phenomenon. Low pay for a sizeable proportion of those in work and the increasing incidence of marital breakdown are two factors underlying this change in the scale of the problem, but by far the biggest contribution comes from unemployment. This being so, it is in the political economy, and not just in a reactive social policy, that we shall need to search for remedies.

The notion of 'the problem family' has a long and not particularly honourable history in social work theory and practice. Lowe and Tasker's essay examines the fuzziness of the concept and they conclude that it usually contains, implicitly or explicitly, some element of 'trouble for agencies': problem families are those that make 'excessive' or 'awkward' demands, usually upon several agencies. It received a new lease of life from the associated idea of a 'cycle of disdvantage', despite the lack of good evidence for the existence of such cross-generational transmission of disadvantage. One of the perennial dilemmas of social work (and social policy) is highlighted from this perspective: are problems to be seen as evidence of individual pathology, and hence to be 'treated'; or as generated by inequalities in a social structure which needs to be altered?

Similar issues of causation, and the consequences for intervention, are raised in Gough and Boddy's chapter on violence. From one standpoint, therapy may be seen 'at best as palliative and at worst as reinforcing inequalities particularly when they "blame the victim"' (p.84). On the other hand the field worker has to take the situation as s/he finds it in responding to the needs of the client, be that client an individual or a family. The dilemmas then are to respect the privacy and autonomy of families while protecting individual members; both parents and children have rights, for example, and the decisions on when and how to intervene are made more difficult when agencies fail to provide adequate guidelines for procedure.

In one sense, interventions in the case of 'loss' of or from the family seem more straightforward: in bereavement, for example, there is no 'perpetrator' and no 'victim'. Other forms of loss, however, may result from decisions taken by family members. The papers by Jenkins and Chisholm emphasise the complexities of family dynamics and the consequences of different modes of response. Jenkins counsels against regarding every aspect of human difficulty as 'loss', while acknowledging the usefulness of the concept in understanding the tensions that arise at different phases of a family's development. One of the consequences of loss, whether of a person or of the functions of that person, is an alteration in the configuration of the family: bereavement leaves, both literally and metaphorically, an empty chair at the table and families may need help to work out whether the chair should be removed, left empty, or filled by someone else. The structure of relationships has been more or less radically damaged and repair involves all family members. Relief, then, may require a realignment of family roles and this may be difficult to achieve through therapy or casework with the presenting client alone.

Indeed, as Chisholm points out, some family therapists would not even assess the referred client/patient on the grounds that such an initial focus on the individual may 'militate against a shift...to it being seen as a family problem and because of the risk of collusion' (p.131). The perspective which is likely to be supported by most therapists, however, would suggest that assessments should be made of the referred individual, the family as a system and the wider social context in which the unit is embedded, in order to identify the point(s) at which intervention is likely to be most effective. This may be a counsel of perfection, though, since time and other resources are likely to be in short supply, and research-based evidence on the effectiveness of different modes of treatment is limited.

This theme of the appropriate form of intervention is central to the final contribution by Hunt. Using the problems associated with, or subsumed under the rubric of 'marital difficulties', she shows how different phases of change or dissolution in a family may require different forms of response. There are no easy solutions: ventilation of grievances may help facilitate honest communication or reinforce the negative features of the relationship, for example, and the guidelines and procedures, so necessary for the smooth functioning of departments and the sense of security of field-workers, may inhibit the openness of approach and empathic understanding of the client's world which are so vital for a successful outcome.

This does not mean, however, that the worker can adopt a completely pragmatic approach. Indeed it emerges from the literature that interventions need to be structured so that goals are agreed and the division of responsibility made clear. The task remains of matching the method of intervention to the problems being addressed, a task which is made more difficult by the relatively under-developed state of 'practice theory'. Linda Hunt's discussion of different forms of family therapy and networking is most useful in this context, not least because she raises the question, so often glossed over, of what constitutes 'the family' or 'network' for the purpose at hand. Practitioners, I would argue, can never afford to take the answer to this question for granted.

This collection of essays will not have answered, and should not be expected to answer, the question posed in the title – 'context or client?' We hope, however, to have provided the reader with a reasoned discussion of some of the evidence which bears upon the problem and of the factors which the practitioner might bear in mind in deciding how and where to intervene.

Part 1: Background

Family Structure and Behaviour in Britain since 1945

Christopher Turner

INTRODUCTION

'Family' is a commonplace term in everyday use in Britain. Highly generalised notions of 'the family' play an important part in public discourse. Ideas about what the family ought to be are projected strongly through legislation, central and local government policies, religious and humanistic doctrine, and the mass media. In addition, the organisation of production and distribution of goods and services, labour market processes, and consumption patterns, reflect fundamental ideas and taken-for-granted assumptions about family structure and behaviour. The net result is a set of public images and cultural stereotypes of 'the family' in which there is a subtle and shifting blend of myth and reality. There is also a private side to 'the family'. Few people lack experience of direct participation in at least some aspects of family life. Private, personal, idiosyncratic, and intimate experiences provide a basis from which individuals derive a variety of different meanings and values relating to 'the family'. The interplay of public images and private meanings is associated with the use of complex multi-layered conceptions of 'the family' in everyday life. These are by no means always consistent, and can and do give rise to contradictory expectations both within and between groups. Nevertheless it does mean that common frameworks for discussion, debate and the crystallisation of expectations about family structure and behaviour are created at the grass roots level.

This chapter is concerned with major changes in family structure and behaviour which have occurred in Britain since 1945, and with the expansion and development of our knowledge of different aspects of domestic relations in recent years. Broad shifts in household structure and composition are first discussed, and provide an overview which helps to set the discussion of more detailed empirical studies in context. Some attempt is made to indicate the richness and variety of current work on diverse aspects of domestic behaviour. The lack of agreement on any unifying theoretical perspective, however, makes it extremely difficult to capitalise on the theoretical insights to be gained from these studies. Therefore, a presentation strategy has been adopted which relies on the use of specific works to illustrate and explore different types of approach to explanation. This is followed by a short section on public images of the family which draws attention to the influence of the law and the media in modelling family behaviour.

HOUSEHOLD STRUCTURE AND COMPOSITION

A majority of households in modern Britain consist of a core of members related by ties of marriage and/or filiation (i.e. parent-child relations). Patterns of household composition can be analysed in terms of developmental cycles in domestic groups. The overwhelming majority of newly married couples establish their own homes shortly before or after marriage. Households increase in size with the birth of children, and lose members through death, divorce, and young people leaving the parental home. In addition, many households are expanded at some time in the developmental cycle by the addition of relatives, friends, or lodgers, who do not belong to the core unit of parents and children. Such additions are often of relatively short duration. Basic information on population in private households is given in Table 1. The broad trends in household composition are summarised in Table 2.

Changing demographic patterns have a marked impact on household structure and composition. Since 1945 marriage rates have remained consistently high with between 89 and 95 per cent of individuals marrying at least once by the age of 45. The crude death rate has declined. The main impact comes from a dramatic reduction in the rate of infant mortality, which has halved. There has been a corresponding increase in the average expectancy of life. The birth rate has fluctuated, peaking immediately after the war, and again in the early 1960s. There was a further mini-boom in the late 1970s, but the overall trend has been downwards. The average number of births per married woman at age 45, and the interval between the birth of the first-born and last-born, have both declined[8]. Divorce and remarriage rates have increased spectacularly[9]. Current projections suggest that one in three current marriages is likely to end in divorce compared with one in seven just after the war.

Increasing prosperity, both in terms of income levels and the availability of

TABLE 1

Great Britain: population and household size from census data 1951-1981 (thousands)

	Census year			
	1951	1961	1971	1981
Total population	48,854	51,284	53,979	54,285
Private households	14,482	16,189	18,317	19,493
Population in private households				
No.	45,528	50,011	52,848	52,772
Percentage	93.2%	97.5%	97.9%	97.2%
Average no. of persons per private household	3.14	3.09	2.89	2.71

Sources: [1,2,3,4,5,6,7]

housing, has been an important factor in opening up the range of available options for household structure. The greater purchasing power of incomes at all social class levels coincides with a significant decline in the proportion of disposable income spent on accommodation. The only exception is among the poorest households, which are eligible for housing benefit and rate support grants. State housing policies have also had a major influence. In the immediate post-war period, housing shortages had some impact on the composition of domestic groups, but the commitment in the 1945 White Paper on housing to 'a separate dwelling for every family which desires to have one' became a cornerstone of social policy [10, p.2]. In recent decades housing shortages have not been a significant factor in the formation of composite households. The proportion of households containing the nuclei of two or more core families has declined dramatically from about 13 per cent in 1951 to less than 1 per cent in 1981. Conversely the proportion of one-person households has nearly doubled to over 21 per cent. Despite a failure to harmonise public sector planning with changing patterns of household composition and the demand for different types of housing, and a number of major design problems, local authority housing has become much more widely available[10,11,12]. Private housing markets have responded flexibly, whether to the demand for home ownership, to income guarantees by the

TABLE 2

Britain: percentage of private households by selected types of composition from census data 1951-1981

Types of composition	Census year			
	1951	1961	1971	1981
Solitaries	11.3	11.9	18.1	21.8
Married couples only	21.6	22.5	24.7	24.1
Married couples and unmarried children only	41.5	(43/44)	40.1	36.6
Lone parents and unmarried children only	4.9	(5/6)	5.5	6.5
Composite households	13.7	2.7	1.4	0.9
Others (mainly expanded households)	7	(15.9)	10.2	10.9
Total	100	100	100	100

Figures in brackets are estimates. The 1951 figures for lone parent households, composite households and others are not strictly comparable with those for later years.

Sources: [1,2,3,4,5,6,7]

state, or to the imposition of rent controls in the private rented sector [13,14,15].

The massive increase in the number and proportion of solitaries (people in one-person households) reflects diverse underlying trends. By far the greatest rise in the numbers of solitaries has occurred among the over-sixties. This is in part a straightforward reflection of the changing age distribution of the population as a whole, and the differential survival rates of husbands and wives. However, it is also a product of changing ideas about family obligations towards the elderly, and changing patterns of service provision for the elderly infirm. More elderly people have the material resources to sustain homes of their own. The range and scope of domiciliary services have improved considerably. Economic pressures for 'family' to take in elderly infirm parents have declined, and resistance to moral pressures has increased in certain sectors of the population. The proportion of places in old people's homes and long stay geriatric institutions has not increased significantly, and has certainly declined in relation to levels of incapacity. The rising number of solitaries in the under-25 age category is evidence of an increasing tendency for young people to leave the parental home and to defer or avoid marriage. The least increase in solitaries has occurred in the 25 to 6O age range. There has been an increase in marital breakdown affecting this age group, but this is compensated for by the fact that many of the ensuing one-person households are relatively transient [16,17].

The decline in the proportion of households comprising a nuclear family unit of parents and children is noticeable, but not dramatic – from 40.1 per cent in 1951 to 36.6 per cent in 1981. This is still the predominant form of domestic group. The decline is primarily an effect of the changing age structure of the population. Although there are fewer couples in the childbearing age range, more of them are living in households with unmarried children. A few such households involve a step-parent or adoptive parents. The vast majority, however, live with their own offspring. The behavioural evidence, therefore, suggests that most people have rejected neither marriage nor childrearing.

The proportion of households containing married couples only has increased from 21.6 per cent in 1951 to 24.1 per cent in 1981. There has been an increase in both the number and proportion of such couples in the higher age categories, especially among those over retirement age. These figures clearly reflect the impact of the changing age structure, the shorter time in the developmental cycle of domestic groups being devoted to childrearing, and the fact that some young people are tending to leave the parental home earlier. The decline in the proportion of younger couples living alone is associated with current tendencies for them (1) to marry later and have children sooner after marriage (if not before), (2) to separate more frequently, and (3) to become involved in other non-nuclear family based forms of domestic group more frequently [16,18,19].

Finally it must be noted that there has been a small but steady growth of lone parent households. This applies both to units composed of a lone parent and child/ren, and to units composed of a lone parent, child/ren, and other/s. The increase is associated both with increasing rates of marital breakdown and with deliberate decisions of unmarried mothers to rear their illegitimate infants. The turnover of lone parent households has also increased. This is associated with higher rates of remarriage, and means that an increasing number of households are experiencing this pattern at some juncture [20]. A substantial proportion of lone parent households are among the lowest 20 per cent in terms of household income, and as such among the modern poor in British society [21,22,23].

These broad patterns of change in household structure and composition are in one sense an aggregate product of individual decisions and actions concerning marriage, homemaking, childbearing, commensality, and cohabitation. They can also be seen as the outcomes of continuing processes of interpersonal negotiation. The cumulative effects of individual choice and interpersonal negotiation result in changes in structure which in turn have their own aggregate effects on behaviour by changing the nature of structural limitations and constraints on behaviour. For example, the combined impact of changing demographic patterns, rising prosperity, and shifts in housing and family policy has resulted in the creation of a wider range of viable options for the majority of the population concerning patterns of household structure and composition. Increasing freedom of choice about domestic arrangements is also related to significant shifts in cultural values. Both public and private expectations about domestic arrangements and family relations reflect an increasingly pragmatic approach.

THE PRIVATE ASPECT OF FAMILY RELATIONS

Social scientists know considerably more about the public than the private face of family relations. It is extremely difficult for outsiders to penetrate the veil of privacy which surrounds marital and parent-child relations. Many family theorists believe that it is precisely this quality of 'invisibility', of not always being on public show, which makes relations within long-lasting domestic groups so important in advanced industrial societies. There are several ways of expressing and experiencing this aspect of domestic life. It may be associated with strong feelings of security and personal well-being – having a base in which to unwind, relax, and just be yourself, and being with people whom you trust in a taken-for-granted way. This type of perspective emphasises the family as a 'haven in a heartless world' [24]. Alternatively, private domestic life may be viewed as having a more sinister character. Studies of the captive housewife and housebound mother show how it is possible to develop a sense of being trapped within a small private world [25]. Recent work on marital violence and child abuse has raised both analytical and social policy issues concerned with the unacceptable face of domestic relations [26,27].

Domestic relations are essentially negotiated relations, despite the fact that what goes on in the privacy of the household is often strongly influenced by cultural stereotypes and external social forces. This negotiated aspect of social order in the small group context of household living means that patterns of behaviour in domestic groups can be extremely varied, whatever the face presented to the outside world. The growing range of in-depth studies of various aspects of family behaviour illustrates this extremely well. Such studies, however, tend to be small scale. Therefore, it is difficult to assess their representativeness. Nevertheless there has been substantial progress both in extending the scope and content of our empirically based knowledge of various aspects of family life, and in the development of theoretical insights and explanatory models.

Several studies have contributed to our knowledge of diverse aspects of household developmental cycles. Leonard[28] has produced the first major study of courtship, weddings and starting off married life. Oakley has contributed to the understanding of childbirth by reporting and analysing mothers' accounts of their experiences of pregnancy, childbirth, and caring for an infant[29], and by comparing and contrasting them with medical models[30]. The early work of the Newsons[31,32] on patterns of infant care has been supplemented by Backet's study of the development and negotiation of parenthood[33]. Mitchell has explored the ways in which husbands and wives sought help both informally and through formal services during the process of marital breakdown[34], and has also produced the first major British study which compares children's feelings and experiences with those of their divorcing parents[35]. Hart[36] has examined the causes and consequences of divorce, and developed a perceptive analysis of the processes of transition involved in marital breakdown and post-divorce readjustment. There have also been studies focussed on how families cope with specific problems such as childlessness[37], the care of handicapped children[38,39], the process of seeking help with marital problems[40], and dementia[41].

Other studies have concentrated more heavily on the relationship between work and family. Oakley[42] has tackled the subject of housework by examining the satisfactions and dissatisfactions of housewives with the nature and conditions of their unpaid domestic work, and contrasted feelings about housework with feelings about being a housewife. This was followed by a series of papers exploring different aspects of dependence and exploitation in work and marriage[43]. The Rapoports[44,45] have examined the organisation of dual career households, and the different coping strategies adopted. Finch[46], building on the earlier work of the Pahls[47], has addressed the issue of the incorporation of wives into their husbands' careers, and stressed the importance of the active participation of wives in shaping their own lives in meaningful ways within current cultural and structural limitations and constraints. Pollert[48] has documented the attitudes and experiences of female manual workers whose jobs are under threat, towards both work and home. Fagin and Little[49] have demonstrated the cultural and structural significance of employment to family life, and have presented detailed case materials on clinical depression, the illness of children, and marital problems in families of the unemployed.

These empirical studies are remarkable for the richness of materials which they present, whether based on questionnaire surveys, in-depth interviews, participant observation, or some combination of these. However, theoretical perspectives from which they have been written are enormously varied. The task of theoretical integration is daunting and there is still much work to be done in this field. Nevertheless it is possible to illustrate some of the progress already made by reference to work on marital relations and child development.

Bott[50] pioneered the analysis of marital division of labour in Britain, defining patterns of segregated, complementary, or joint relations according to the degree to which responsibilities for domestic tasks were shared and whether activities were carried out jointly or not. Subsequent writers have demonstrated that sharing may take place with respect to some activities, but not others[51,52]. The explanation of these different patterns of marital relations presents a number of problems. One approach is to start by examining the extent to which changing patterns of marital relations can be attributed to long term secular changes in the social and economic structure. Alternatively, it is possible to begin from the participant's social construction and understanding of specific family relations, and to attempt to assess how objective external circumstances and shared social constructions of those circumstances, generated through interaction and wider forms of communication, impinge upon social behaviour.

Young and Willmott[53] attempted to use the first type of approach to interpret the growth of the 'symmetrical family'. Their general argument is that industrialisation and technological development set in motion fundamental changes in family structure. There was a major nineteenth century shift in which the household became less a unit of production and more a unit of consumption, economically dependent upon the participation of the breadwinner in the labour market. Consequently marital relations became increasingly segregated. More recently the cumulated impact of technological change has worked in the reverse direction. Higher per capita productivity levels have led to a greater prosperity and higher material standards of living for families at all social class levels. With the development of the economy married women have been drawn increasingly into the labour market. The contraceptive revolution has made the choice of whether or not to have children a viable option. New technologies have done much to change the nature of housework. The net effect has been a move towards financial partnership and the desegregation of sex roles in marriage.

This type of general argument is open to a series of criticisms. It tends to ignore cultural as opposed to social structural effects. It gives far too little attention to the processes involved in producing changing patterns of marital relations. It is concerned with the dominant trend, and offers no explanation for domestic relations which go against the current trend. Nevertheless it does draw together a series of arguments about macro-structural effects which have a definite place in the explanation of family behaviour.

Askham's work [54] illustrates the second type of approach. She starts from the theme of the contribution of marriage to identity formation. Partners' perspectives on the impact of knowing and talking to each other, separate and joint activity, perceived constraints on behaviour in marriage, changes in self-concept and associated behaviour patterns, and involvement in external personal relations are explored. She centres her analysis on the extent to which marriage can simultaneously contribute to a developing sense of identity, yet in and of itself generate a sense of stability for each partner. On the basis of the self-report data from the 20 couples in her study, she suggests that 'marriage is in many ways a compromise between stability-maintaining and identity-upholding behaviour, and that on the whole married couples perform this balancing act skilfully' (p.183). The importance of the study rests on the fact that the explanation of marital relations depends upon taking account of (1) participants' understandings of processes of marital interaction and the reciprocal spillover effects between marital and other activities; (2) the ways in which individual development, changing resources, and changing involvement in social relations may either be congruent or destructive of the marital relationship; (3) recognition of the complexity of the interplay of both personal feelings and cognitive assessments in the social construction of an ongoing marital relationship; and (4) acknowledgement of the impact of wider cultural meanings attributed to marriage and of vicarious experiences of other people's marriages in influencing evaluations and interpretations of one's own marriage.

This type of theoretical approach, in combination with the analysis of structural effects, offers a way forward in the analysis of family structure and behaviour. The crucial link between the two might be forged by developing the range of ideas about ways in which interaction in interpersonal networks reflects structural and cultural effects and influences personal behaviour [50,55].

The work on reproduction, childrearing and parenting is characterised by similar problems of explanation. One strand of research depends upon establishing broad patterns of association. For example, the results of longitudinal studies started in 1946 [56,57] and 1958 [58] respectively have clearly and unequivocally established a pattern of compounded advantage which is associated with social class. Crudely summarised, the findings indicate that the greater the household resources, and the greater the parental interest in a child's development and personal achievements, the more likely a child is to relate positively to teachers and the greater a child's educational achievements are likely to be. The overall statistical patterns, however, conceal significant variations. The evidence indicates that when the social pressures of home, school and peer group exhibit a high degree of consistency and mutual reinforcement, the outcome is more easily predictable. When social pressures are more diverse, as is often, though by no means necessarily, the case with children from poorer homes and lone parent households, the outcomes are far less predictable. This type of approach is useful for setting the context for more detailed research into patterns and processes of child development.

Specialist studies of the impact of residential care, fostering, and adoption on child development offer a further contribution to our theoretical understanding. The insights developed from the work of Skeels[59] in the United States in the 1930s have been substantiated and elaborated in a range of British studies[60,61,62]. The impact of genetic endowment, of the level of nutrition and physical care, and of the quality of social relations upon the development of individual identity, personal abilities, and social skills is now firmly established, although the complex processes by which the effects are achieved are less well-understood.

The crucial part played by warm continuous relationships with 'parent figures' in infant and child development is well recognised. This type of relationship is particularly important in helping a child to crystallise both a positive sense of identity and a capacity for developing and sustaining personal relations with others in later life. From the children's perspective, such relationships need to allow for the growth of autonomy within the context of emotional security. This implies a need for reciprocal adjustment on the part of parent figures. The recent work of Triseliotis and Russell[63] confirms the results of earlier studies. The comparison was between experiences of growing up in children's homes as opposed to adoptive families. They found that adoptees' identity was mostly built round their adoptive families, and reported that:

> 'The qualities in the parents which were perceived as having contributed to the success of adoption were love, closeness, warmth, stability, confidence in parenting, openness and honesty about adoption, and encouragement and support' (p.181).

Adoptees who did not develop warm emotional relations with their new parents, or who felt that there was no way they could meet parental aspirations, reflected much lower levels of satisfaction with their upbringing, and had more problems of personal adjustment in later life. The majority of adoptees had positive feelings towards experiences of growing up, whereas the reverse was true for those who spent a substantial period in residential care, especially when they experienced a lack of individualised care, felt that they had not received explanations of what was happening to them or why, and sensed that they were stigmatised by outsiders. Conversely, the few with strong positive feelings about their residential experience emphasised their appreciation of continuity of relations with caring staff, their enjoyment of a relaxed and informal atmosphere in the children's home, and their receipt of individual attention. The complex relationships between identity-formation, interpersonal interaction, and the impact of the immediate domestic environment are well-illustrated in this study.

Macintyre [64] in *Single and Pregnant* develops the pattern of analysis even further. Her interpretation of pregnancy careers takes account of the interplay of (1) the pregnant woman's definition of her situation; (2) the form and content of support for or challenges to her plans or feelings in face-to-face interaction with others; (3) the contingent way in which situational factors such as the timing of her realisation of pregnancy, the attitudes of the particular general practitioner with whom she happened to be registered, or the views of the gynaecologist to whom she was referred, impinge upon her behavioural options; (4) the 'successive limited comparisons' style of decision making used throughout the pregnancy career by the major parties involved; (5) the matrix of moral values which are brought into play by coalitions of individuals involved both directly and indirectly in successive decisions; and (6) objective measures of material resources available and the patterning and structuring of social relations.

PUBLIC IMAGES OF THE FAMILY, THE LAW, AND THE MEDIA

Family imagery is well-developed in British society. The public images of 'the family' presented via the law and the mass media appear to be of particular importance. Legal images of the family simultaneously constitute a model of and a model for socially acceptable family behaviour. Such models tend to be conservative. They serve as practical guides to prescribed, permitted, and prohibited behaviour. Changes tend to reflect rather than anticipate existing problems. They also tend to evolve in a piecemeal fashion. From time to time there is a major consolidation and tidying up of contradictions in the models, but for the most part changes stem from attempts to devise new solutions to existing problems.

The concept of family relations as a bundle of rights, duties and obligations reached its apogee in mid-nineteenth century Britain. The basic assumptions underlying Christian models were combined with ideas about the ownership and control of private property to develop a tight jural model of the family as a basic property holding and controlling unit. Since then, there has been a steady loosening of the various legal strands which emphasised and reinforced the authority of the father/husband/head of household, his rights in reproduction, the housekeeping and childrearing responsibilities of the wife/mother, and the privileges of legitimate children.

Since 1945, legislation has tended to reinforce and strengthen the rights of individuals at the expense of family obligations. The major changes are those associated with the recognition of marital breakdown, and with parental rights and the best interests of the child[65,66,67,68]. The areas in which the liberalisation of family law has had least impact are those of taxation and social security[69,70]. Legal assumptions about family rights, duties and obligations are especially conservative in those fields.

The pervasiveness of media images has been increasing over recent decades. The main reasons for this are not difficult to discern. The mass media project a kaleidoscopic array of images concerning almost every aspect of domestic life. There is something on offer to cater to almost every taste. The greatest changes have occurred with and are attributable to the advent of television. It has penetrated into 97 per cent of all households. As a medium it has a power to capture interest and excite imagination. Interestingly, whatever the presentation format – news, sitcom, chat show, classic 'theatre' or 'film', documentary, or advertisements – allusions, imagery and vivid vignettes with family associations abound. It displays life, and family life in particular, in all its richness and variety. It also goes further and creates images and models in the realm of phantasy, which may appeal to people, and may even influence behaviour. Television, therefore, offers a profusion of potential models of and models for behaviour in a wide range of both 'realistic' and extremely bizarre situations. There are surprisingly few aspects of family or domestic relations that the average teenage viewer will not have come across on television. Glimpses will have been offered into multiple facets of sex and reproduction, of marital harmony and conflict, of the extremes of family violence, and of parental indulgence and authority. A welter of different role models for father, husband, wife, mother, son, daughter, brother, sister, and other types of family relations will have been provided. Information of varying reliability and accuracy on ethnic differences, and on almost every conceivable type of health and social problem and their possible family implications, will have been encountered. It is somewhat surprising that the impact of legal models of appropriate family structure and behaviour, and of media imagery concerning domestic relations, has not been subjected to more rigorous analysis. Their significance and importance tend to be taken for granted rather than thoroughly investigated. The multi-layered analytical approach illustrated by the work of Macintyre[64] would appear to be eminently adaptable for this type of research.

CONCLUSIONS

The interpretation of changing patterns of family behaviour is problematic. On the one hand it is necessary to acknowledge that particular structural and cultural contexts exert strong influences on domestic organisation and family behaviour, both in the sense of offering strong supports for certain patterns of interaction, resource use, and individual social constructions of reality, and in the sense of constituting major obstacles to be overcome by those with the will and imagination to develop different life-styles. On the other hand it must also be acknowledged that individuals are active participants in shaping the nature and meaning of the domestic relations in which they are involved. As they mature, they develop a capacity to recognise and choose among options and to negotiate over the course which their lives may follow. However, this is not to suggest that they are free agents who can ride roughshod over structural and cultural forces, or that as biological organisms they are not subject to a whole range of external contingencies. The weight to be attributed to different types of explanatory factor, and the ways in which different factors interact to produce particular effects, are still a theoretical minefield. The fundamental theoretical issues are how to assess the contribution of idiosyncratic initiatives, as opposed to social influences; how to determine the extent to which perceptions and social constructions of reality serve to create, as opposed to reflect and reinforce, patterns of behaviour; and how to distinguish the relative strength of different cultural and social structural limitations and constraints.

References

1. Registrar General. *Census of Great Britain 1951: one per cent sample tables*. H.M.S.O., 1962.
2. Registrar General. *Census of England and Wales 1961: household composition tables England and Wales*. H.M.S.O., 1964.
3. Registrar General. *Census of England and Wales 1971: household composition tables*. H.M.S.O., 1975.

4. Registrar General for Scotland. *Census of Scotland 1961: household composition tables*. H.M.S.O., 1964.

5. Registrar General for Scotland. *Census of Scotland 1975 : household composition tables*. H.M.S.O., 1975.

6. O.P.C.S. *Census 1981: household composition tables England and Wales*. H.M.S.O., 1983.

7. Registrar General for Scotland. *Census 1981: household composition tables Scotland*. H.M.S.O., 1984.

8. Central Statistical Office. *Social Trends No. 14*. H.M.S.O., 1984.

9. Thornes, B. & Collard, J. *Who Divorces?* Routledge and Kegan Paul, 1979.

10. White Paper. *Housing*. H.M.S.O., Cmnd. 6609, 1945.

11. English, J. (Ed.) *The Future of Council Housing*. Croom Helm, 1982.

12. Merrett, S. *State Housing in Britain*. Routledge and Kegan Paul, 1979.

13. Department of Environment. *Housing Policy: a Consultative Document*. H.M.S.O., Cmnd. 6851, 1977.

14. Scottish Office. *Scottish Housing: a Consultative Document*. H.M.S.O., Cmnd. 6852, 1977.

15. Merrett, S. & Gray, F. *Owner Occupation in Britain*. Routledge and Kegan Paul, 1982.

16. Leete, R. *Changing Patterns of Family Formation and Dissolution in England and Wales 1964-1976*. H.M.S.O., 1979.

17. Leete, R. & Anthony, S. 'Divorce and Remarriage: a Record Linkage Study' *Population Trends*. 16, 1979, 5-11.

18. Brown, A. & Kiernan, K. 'Cohabitation in Great Britain: Evidence from the General Household Survey' *Population Trends*. 25, 1981, 4-10.

19. Holmans, A. 'Housing Careers of Recently Married Couples' *Population Trends*. 24, 1981, 10-14.

20. Leete, R. 'One-parent Families: Numbers and Characteristics' *Population Trends*. 13, 1978, 4-9.

21. Barber, D. *Unmarried Fathers*. Hutchison, 1975.

22. Finer, M. (Chairman). *Report of the Committee on One-parent Families*. H.M.S.O., Cmnd. 5629, 1974.

23. Marsden, D. *Mothers Alone*. Allen Lane, 1969.

24. Lasch, C. *Haven in a Heartless World*. Basic Books, 1977.

25. Gavron, H. *The Captive Wife*. Penguin, 1966.

26. Dobash, R.E. & Dobash, R.P. *Violence Against Wives*. Free Press, 1979.

27. Parton, N. *The Politics of Child Abuse*. Macmillan, 1985.

28. Leonard, D. *Sex and Generation: a Study of Courtship and Weddings*. Tavistock, 1980.

29. Oakley, A. *Becoming a Mother*. Martin Robertson, 1979.

30. Oakley, A. *Women Confined: Towards a Sociology of Childbirth*. Martin Robertson, 1980.

31. Newson, J. & Newson, E. *Infant Care in an Urban Community*. Allen and Unwin, 1963.

32. Newson, J. & Newson, E. *Four Years Old in an Urban Community*. Allen and Unwin, 1968.

33. Backet, K.C. *Mothers and Fathers*. Macmillan, 1982.

34. Mitchell, A.K. *Someone to Turn To: Experiences of Help Before Divorce*. Aberdeen University Press, 1981.

35. Mitchell, A.K. *Children in the Middle*. Tavistock, 1985.

36. Hart, N. *When Marriage Ends: a Study of Status Passage*. Tavistock, 1976.

37. Houghton, D. & Houghton, P. *Coping with Childlessness*. George Allen and Unwin, 1984.

38. Glendinning, C. *Unshared Care*. Routledge and Kegan Paul, 1983.

39. Anderson, E.M. & Spain, B. *The Child with Spina Bifida*. Methuen, 1977.

40. Brannen, J. & Collard, J. *Marriages in Trouble: the Process of Help Seeking*. Tavistock, 1982.

41. Gilleard, C.J. *Living with Dementia: Community Care of the Elderly Mentally Infirm*. Croom Helm, 1984.

42. Oakley, A. *The Sociology of Housework*. Martin Robertson, 1974.

43. Barker, D. & Allen, S. *Dependence and Exploitation in Work and Marriage*. Longman, 1976.

44. Rapoport, R. & Rapoport, R.N. *Dual-Career Families*. Penguin, 1971.

45. Rapoport, R. & Rapoport, R.N. *Dual-Career Families Re-examined*. Martin Robertson, 1975.

46. Finch, J. *Married to the Job: Wives' Incorporation in Men's Work*. George Allen and Unwin, 1983.

47. Pahl, J.I. & Pahl, R.E. *Managers and their Wives*. Penguin, 1972.

48. Pollert, A. *Girls, Wives, Factory Lives*. Macmillan, 1981.

49. Fagin, L. & Little, M. *The Forsaken Families*. Penguin, 1984.

50. Bott, E. *Family and Social Network*. Tavistock, 1957.

51. Platt, J. 'Some Problems of Measuring the Jointness of Conjugal Role Relations' *Sociology*. 3, 1969, 287-297.

52. Edgell, S. *Middle Class Couples: a Study of Segregation , Domination and Inequality in Marriage*. George Allen and Unwin, 1980.

53. Young, M. & Willmott, P. *The Symmetrical Family*. Penguin, 1973.

54. Askham, J. *Identity and Stability in Marriage*. Cambridge University Press, 1984.

55. Turner, C. 'Conjugal Roles and Social Networks' *Human Relations*. 2O, 1967, 121-131.

56. Douglas, J.W.B. *The Home and the School*. MacGibbon and Kee, 1964.

57. Douglas, J.W.B., Ross, J.M. & Simpson, H.R. *All Our Future*. Peter Davies, 1968.

58. Davie, R., Butler, N. & Goldstein, H. *From Birth to Seven*. Longman, 1972.

59. Skeels, H.M. 'Adult Status of Children with Contrasting Early Life Experiences: a Follow-up Study' *Monographs of the Society for Research in Child Development*. 31, 3, 1966.

60. Tizard, B. *Adoption: a Second Chance*. Open Books, 1977.

61. Triseliotis, J. (Ed.) *New Developments in Foster Care and Adoption*. Routledge and Kegan Paul, 1980.

62. Rowe, J., Cain, H., Hundleby, M. & Keane, A. *Long-term Foster Care*. Batsford, 1984.

63. Triseliotis, J. & Russell, J. *Hard to Place*. Heinemann, 1984.

64. Macintyre, S. *Single and Pregnant*. Croom Helm, 1977.

65. Dingwall, R., Eekelaar, J. & Murray, T. *The Protection of Children*. Blackwell, 1983.

66. Maidment, S. *Child Custody and Divorce: the Law in Social Content*. Croom Helm, 1984.

67. Masson, J., Norbury, D. & Chatterton, S.G. *Mine, Yours or Ours? A Study of Step-Parent Adoption*. H.M.S.O., 1983.

68. Murch, M. *Justice and Welfare in Divorce*. Sweet and Maxwell, 1980.

69. Land, H. 'Sex-role Stereotyping in the Social Security and Income Tax Systems'. In Chetwynd, J. & Harnett, O. (Eds.) *The Sex-role System*. Routledge and Kegan Paul, 1978.

70. Secretary of State for Social Services. *Reform of Social Security Vol. III*. H.M.S.O., Cmnd 9515, 1985.

Family Law, Family Courts, and Statutory Duties of Social Work Departments to Families

David Lessels

This article, which is written with a heavy Scots Law bias, has four main aims:

1. to describe how the civil courts in Scotland are organised for the purposes of resolving legal issues relating to the family;
2. to provide an explanation of some of the more important substantive rules of Scots family law that come into play on family breakdown;
3. related to the previously stated aim, to outline some of the legal duties which particular pieces of legislation have placed upon social work departments towards families; and
4. to assess the arguments for the introduction of a Family Court in Scotland.

1. ORGANISATION OF THE CIVIL COURTS

Family law is essentially a corpus of rules governing three different sets of relationship: husband and wife, parent and child, and the relationship of the family to the State. It could be argued that a fourth relationship should be added to this list in the form of persons who cohabit without marrying, but in Scots law at least, very little legal recognition is given to the status of cohabitation, the law almost treating the cohabitees as strangers. Nevertheless, if the law applicable to any of the aforementioned relationships is in dispute, and assuming there is no question of the unresolved dispute raising questions of possible breaches of the criminal law, the matter will normally have to be adjudicated upon by courts of civil jurisdiction, i.e. civil courts. Figure 1 below shows how Scots courts are organised for dealing with civil litigation generally and family litigation particularly. A brief description then follows of the composition, jurisdiction and appellate procedures of each of these courts.

It may seem strange that children's hearings are included in the diagram because strictly speaking it is not a court at all. However, it is a tribunal that so obviously deals with family matters, and whose decisions are subject to review by courts of essentially civil jurisdiction, that it is convenient to explain it along with the other civil courts.

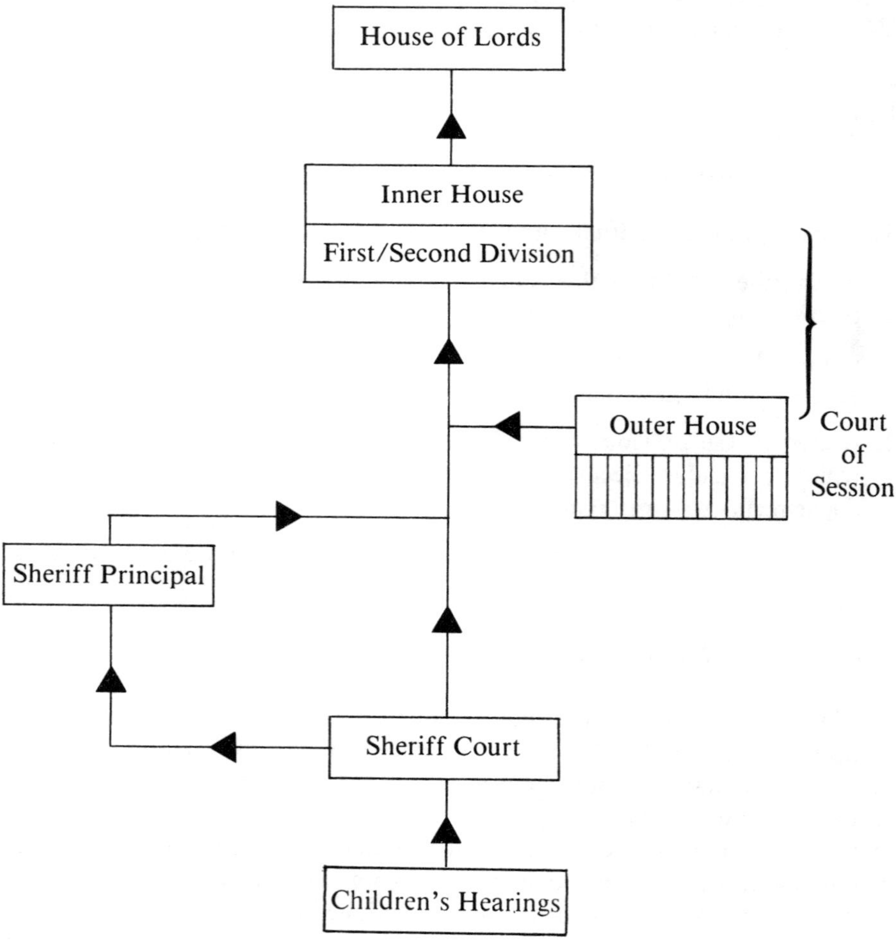

FIGURE 1

House of Lords

This court is Scotland's (and England's) ultimate court of appeal in civil matters, hearing appeals from decisions of the Inner House of the Court of Session. Appeals are heard by legally qualified members of the House who are known as 'Law Lords'. A quorum is three but usually five of their Lordships sit to hear a case. The types of appeal dealt with usually relate to important or difficult questions of law, particularly questions on the meaning of statutory provisions. In *Beagley* v *Beagley* [1], for example, the House had to consider whether a resolution made by a local authority under s.16 of the Social Work (Scotland) Act 1968 (as amended) to assume parental rights over a child, divested the parent of his right to sue for custody of the child; the court held that the resolution did have that effect. Similarly, in the celebrated (English) case of *Lewisham London Borough Council* v. *Lewisham Juvenile Court Justices* [2], the court had to consider, *inter alia*, whether a mother's request for return of her child, who had been taken into 'voluntary' care under the English equivalent of s.15 of the Social Work (Scotland) Act 1968, terminated s.15 'care' so as to bar the passing of a s.16 parental rights resolution; the court *held* that the request *per se* did not terminate 'care'.

Court of Session

This court, which is located in Edinburgh, is Scotland's supreme civil court: it has jurisdiction over the whole of Scotland. The 21 judges who compose it may be regarded as the crème de la crème of the Scottish judiciary; they are appointed from among senior members of the Bar (i.e. the equivalent of English barristers). The court is split into the Inner House and the Outer House.

Inner House: this is divided into the First and Second Division, the former being presided over by the most senior Scottish judge, the Lord President, who sits along with three other judges, while the latter Division is presided over by the Lord Justice-Clerk who is accompanied by another three Court of Session judges. The two Divisions are of equal authority and their main function is to hear appeals from decisions of the Outer House of the Court of Session, the sheriffs and sheriffs principal. Usually three judges sit on an appeal, that number being the quorum. This court's English equivalent is the Court of Appeal (Civil Division).

Outer House: composed of 13 judges, known as Lords Ordinary, each judge sits alone when hearing cases. He does not sit with other judges, although in certain disuptes such as personal injuries actions, he may sit with a jury of 12. The court is almost exclusively a court of first instance; it rarely hears appeals. Apart from having a wide jurisdiction to hear almost any type of civil dispute, e.g. contract, debt, personal injury, property, succession, the court also enjoys a domestic jurisdiction. It is the only court in Scotland which may entertain actions for declarator of marriage (where a party is seeking a declaration that he does enjoy the status of marriage) and actions for declarator of nullity or marriage (where a party seeks a decree that a seeming marriage is not a marriage at all), and actions seeking to establish the legitimacy or illegitimacy of a child. Prior to the Divorce Jurisdiction, Court Fees and Legal Aid (Scotland) Act 1983 coming into force on 1 May 1984, the Court of Session, through the Outer House, jealously guarded its exclusive power to deal with divorces, but from that date the sheriff court was granted concurrent jurisdiction with the Court of Session to hear such cases. Given the comparative speed and cheapness of going to the local sheriff court rather than taking the case to Edinburgh, the Court of Session is likely to become a relatively unimportant divorce tribunal in the future. Other family cases heard by the Lords Ordinary, although not to a significant extent, include actions involving judicial separation of spouses, paternity actions (affiliation proceedings), matrimonial interdicts being sought by the victims of domestic violence, custody of children, and adoptions petitions. This court has an authority and jurisdiction similar to the English High Court.

Sheriff Court

In terms of volume of business the sheriff court is a much more important tribunal than the Court of Session. To facilitate the administration of shrieval justice, Scotland is divided into six Sheriffdoms, each covering a particular area of the country. Each Sheriffdom has at its judicial head a legally qualified sheriff principal who must be a solicitor or an advocate of at least 10 years' standing.

Each Sheriffdom is in turn divided into sheriff court districts, each district covering an area of the Sheriffdom. Each sheriff court district has at least one sheriff who, like the sheriff principal, must be an advocate or solicitor of 10 years' experience.

The sheriff principal's functions are administrative and appellate in nature – administrative in that he is responsible for organising his Sheriffdom and sheriff courts so that they run in an efficient manner, and appellate in that he is empowered to hear appeals from the sheriffs in his Sheriffdom. The court of the sheriff principal, unlike that of the sheriff, is not one of first instance.

The sheriff's civil jurisdiction is almost unlimited. Apart from the small number of cases which only the Court of Session can hear, the sheriff has concurrent jurisdiction with that court to decide almost every type of civil case. Furthermore, it has itself exclusive jurisdiction in actions for debt and damages for claims that are less than £1,000, these actions being heard by the sheriff under what is known as Summary Cause procedure. It is probably fair to say that the sheriff's 'family' case-load is much greater than the Court of Session because not only has the sheriff inherited much of the divorce work previously accorded to the superior court, it is also the obvious court for the person in the street to approach if decisions are required on custody, maintenance, affiliation, separation, and interdicts. Moreover, the sheriff court has important 'miscellaneous' functions to perform that are relevant to the family in such areas as committing patients to mental hospitals under the Mental Health (Scotland) Act 1984, approving adoption petitions under the Adoption (Scotland) Act 1978, and appointing curators *ad bonis* to manage the estates of those unable to do so. The nearest English equivalent of the sheriff court is probably the County Court, but the Sheriff's jurisdiction is even wider than that tribunal because he can also deal with cases that in England are heard in the Magistrate's Court and High Court.

Appeals from decisions of the sheriff can normally be taken either to the sheriff principal or directly to the Inner House of the Court of Session and thereafter, if need be, up to the House of Lords. A fuller discussion of the court system in Scotland, including criminal courts, can be found in Paterson and Bates [3], while Zander [4] provides a succinct description of the English courts.

Children's Hearings

Introduced by the Social Work (Scotland) Act 1968, Part III, the children's hearing system is concerned with children who may be in need of compulsory measures of care. The hearing is conducted before three lay persons, one of whom must be a woman, and cases are brought before them by an individual appointed by the local authority who is designated the 'Reporter'. The children who are subject to the jurisdiction of the hearing must normally be under 16, but in certain circumstances the hearing's jurisdiction extends to children up to 18. There are 11 grounds on which the Reporter may refer a case to the hearing to consider whether the child concerned is in need of compulsory measures of care, including 'he is beyond the control of his parent', 'lack of parental care is likely to cause him unnecessary suffering or seriously to impair his health or development', 'he has committed an offence': s.32, Social Work (Scotland) Act 1968. Should the child accept the ground for referral, the hearing proceeds to dispose of the case, e.g. by imposing a supervision requirement placing the child in a residential establishment. If the ground for referral is not accepted by the child the matter must be put before the sheriff who will decide if the ground is established. If it is, he will remit the case back to the hearing for disposal. Appeals can be made against the decision of the hearing to the sheriff, and thereafter in limited circumstances to the Court of Session: s.50 of the 1968 Act. For further reading on the working of the children's hearing system see Martin and Murray[5]. The different English approach to dealing with juvenile offenders through Juvenile Courts is discussed in Hoggett[6].

2. FAMILY LAW AND FAMILY BREAKDOWN

Cretney, an English lawyer, could have been speaking for Scotland as well when he said[7]:

> 'Family law has grown in quantity and extent enormously in recent years. This is partly because it has increasingly had to deal with the consequences of the breakdown of family relationships; and partly because the State has increasingly been prepared to interfere to make proper arrangements for children who are not adequately provided for.'

The legislative activity in Scots Law over the past 30 years bears out Cretney's assertion, what with the passing of the Matrimonial Proceedings (Children) Act 1958, the hugely important Social Work (Scotland) Act 1968, the Children Act 1975, the Divorce (Scotland) Act 1976, the Adoption (Scotland) Act 1978, the Matrimonial Homes (Family Protection) (Scotland) Act 1981, the Health and Social Services and Social Security Adjudications Act 1983 ('HASSASSAA'), and the Foster Children (Scotland) Act 1984. Many of these statutes have, in turn, spawned their own delegated legislation and occasional Codes of Practice such as the one made under HASSASSAA concerning parents' access to their children who are in local authority care[8]. And the legislative reforms continue apace: the Family Law (Scotland) Bill 1985, which at the time of writing is near to receiving the Royal Assent, will produce fundamental changes in the law governing the award of financial provisions on divorce, while in the not too distant future reforms in the law regarding the illegitimate child are likely[9] [10].

It is obviously not possible, nor desirable, in a work of this scope, to present a detailed, comprehensive analysis of how the statutes mentioned above, as well as all the other rules of family law, respond to the 'consequences of the breakdown of family relationships'; the reader desiring that degree of knowledge should consult specialist books, e.g. [11] and [12], and to the increasing periodical literature on the subject, e.g. [13-16]. However, it may prove helpful to give a general explanation of some of the more important legal rules that could, and often do, come into play when the family relationships fracture. The rules selected for consideration are those relating to a) divorce, b) custody of children on divorce, and c) children in local authority care. Generally speaking, Scots Law is similar to English Law in each of these areas; differences that do exist tend to be of a procedural rather than substantive nature. Readers wishing to know the precise English Law on a particular family law point should refer to the recognised books, e.g. [17-19].

a) Divorce

Before the passing of the Divorce (Scotland) Act 1976, Scots divorce law was based on notions of the matrimonial offence. A spouse could only obtain a decree if the other spouse had committed a matrimonial offence in the form of adultery, cruelty, desertion, sodomy or bestiality; incurable insanity was also a ground. The 1976 Act, which was based largely on the English Divorce Reform Act 1969, changed the law by declaring in s.1[1] that 'irretrievable breakdown of marriage is to be the sole ground for divorce'. Such phraseology made the Act appear very progressive for it implied that the idea of the matrimonial offence was being expunged from divorce law, and that any marriage which had broken down irretrievably could be dissolved[20]. But such an inference was quite misleading because the Act went on to say that 'irretrievable breakdown' shall be taken to be established if any of five grounds are established: (1) the defender's adultery; (2) the defender had 'behaved (whether or not as a result of mental abnormality and whether such behaviour had been active or passive) in such a way that the pursuer cannot reasonably be expected to cohabit with the defender'; (3) the defender's desertion for two years; (4) two years' non-cohabitation between the spouses, the defender consenting to divorce; and (5) five years' non-cohabitation between the spouses. These are therefore the grounds for divorce – not 'irretrievable breakdown of marriage', a phrase whose otioseness was neatly captured by an eminent Law Lord, Lord Simon, who said[20]:

'It is perfectly easy to put a quite nonsensical word like

"abracadabra" in place of "irretrievable breakdown" and the clause would have no different effect.'

The present grounds for divorce are accordingly a combination of the old matrimonial offence grounds (with 'cruelty' being replaced by the more flexible 'unreasonable behaviour' provision) and the two new 'no fault' grounds involving two and five years' non-cohabitation.

The number of marriages ended by divorce has increased markedly over the past 20 years. In 1963, for example, the Court of Session granted 2,218 decrees of divorce. By 1973, that figure had gone up to 7,098, and in 1983 a total of 13,227 divorces were awarded[21]. While it is difficult to predict whether divorces will continue to increase, what is certain is that the sheriff court with its recently acquired concurrent jurisdiction to hear divorce actions, will proceed to become 'the' divorce tribunal in Scotland, and probably a busy one at that.

The statistics are also interesting in indicating the ground upon which decree of divorce is granted. The figures for 1981-1983 are shown below[21]:

		Ground of Divorce				
Year	*Total Divorces*	*Adultery*	*Desertion*	*Behaviour*	*2 years non-cohab.*	*5 years non-cohab.*
1981	9887	1710	230	4140	2437	1370
1982	11275	1879	244	4816	2812	1524
1983	13227	1789	200	4674	4214	2350

'Unreasonable behaviour' is the ground most likely to be the basis of the decree, but the 'no fault' grounds have fully justified their introduction into Scots divorce law, particularly the two-year non-cohabitation ground which in 1983 came close to overtaking 'unreasonable behaviour' as the most 'popular' divorce ground. From a conciliation point of view it is perhaps disappointing that 'unreasonable behaviour' retains its pre-eminence, because, as Eekelaar and Clive found[22], when the old 'cruelty' ground was relied upon this tended to produce hostility between the parties, resulting in greater difficulty for the couple to reach agreement on arrangements affecting the children, such as access and maintenance.

Also worth noting is that the vast majority of divorce actions – about 96 per cent in 1982[23] – are undefended on the merits, i.e. there is no dispute that the divorce ground is established; although there could obviously be defences entered on other aspects of the action, such as custody of children, access, and financial settlements. Indeed it is probably these issues, rather than the divorce grounds themselves, which pose the greatest practical problems in contemporary family law. Reforms in the *substantive* grounds for divorce have been joined in the past seven years by significant *procedural* innovations which have improved the operation of the divorce law. Firstly, as already mentioned, the sheriff court has been given concurrent jurisdiction with the Court of Session to hear divorces[24]. Secondly, all undefended divorce actions can now be disposed of without the necessity of the pursuer having to appear personally in court. While the pursuer must still prove his case, evidence can be on the basis of affidavits, i.e. sworn statements. Thirdly, a simplified 'do-it-yourself' procedure has been introduced for undefended cases in the two and five year non-cohabitation divorce grounds, provided there are no children of the marriage under 16, that neither spouse is claiming a financial provision on divorce, and neither spouse suffers from mental disorder[12]. The new 'D.I.Y.' procedure appears to be working well[25], and it would be surprising if it is not eventually extended (like England) to cover all undefended divorce cases. The fourth innovation, which in Scotland is still in its infancy but which shows great potential for helping to reduce some of the bitterness arising from divorce, is the establishment of conciliation services; more will be said on these later.

b) Custody of Children on Divorce

Annually a large number of children get caught up in the divorce process. In 1983, for example, there were more than 11,000 children (under the age of 16) affected by the divorces granted that year[21]. The figures for the previous two years were of the same order.

What protection does the law give to all these children who are casualties of their parents' divorces? The legal system has bestowed, particularly through the Matrimonial Proceedings (Children) Act 1958, a wide range of powers and duties upon the courts in looking after the interests of children, defined in this context as children under 16. Section 8(1) of that Act provides that the court shall not grant decree of divorce unless it is satisfied that suitable arrangements have been made for the care and upbringing of the child. To satisfy itself as to the proposed arrangements the court can instruct a reporter, who is normally a social worker or advocate, to provide a report on the circumstances of the child and the proposed arrangements (s.11). In any custody case, the court is enjoined by s.1 of the Guardianship of Infants Act 1925 to regard 'the welfare of the child as the first and paramount consideration'; the child's interests are therefore put before those of its parents. In disposing of a custody application, the court will normally grant custody to one of the parents but it can also make an award in favour of other persons, e.g. a grandparent. The non-custodial parent can apply for access, but whether it will be awarded is determined by the 'welfare of the child' test. In granting custody, the court may order that the child should be under the supervision of a local authority, and in circumstances where the court believes it is undesirable for either parent to have the child, it can commit the care of the child to the local authority: ss. 10 and 12 of the 1958 Act.

While the above summary might suggest that the courts play a very active role in protecting the child's interests the reality is somewhat different. Eekelaar and Clive's study showed [22] that only a small percentage of custody (and access) cases were disputed (around 7 per cent), and that in general the parties made their own arrangements about custody, which arrangements were usually accepted by the courts. The researchers found that in both defended and undefended actions the courts preferred to maintain the *status quo* rather than upset a settled relationship: in only 0.8 per cent of the cases was there a change of residence. An interesting quantitative difference was found between English and Scottish courts in the use made of welfare reports under, what in Scotland, is s.11 of the 1958 Act (supra). There was a greater tendency for the English courts to use them: a court welfare officer's report was available in 8 per cent of the uncontested cases and 53 per cent of the contested; in Scotland only 3 per cent of the cases were remitted to a reporter, and these were all contested cases. Courts invariably gave effect to the recommendations in the report. One wonders whether when the sheriff court gets into 'full swing' with its recently acquired divorce jurisdiction it will be more willing to use welfare reports than the Court of Session (where Eekelaar and Clive carried out their study). Seale opines that there is likely to be an increase in the number of reports called [26], and there are also indications in her study that some sheriffs may be more inclined than Lords Ordinary to call reports in undefended cases.

While ultimately the welfare reports may not affect the actual custody arrangement, i.e. the *status quo* is maintained, Eekelaar in another study [27], and summarised in [28], found that in carrying out his investigative duties for the court, the welfare officer, who is a probation officer assigned to the court, played a useful part in improving parents' attitudes towards each other and towards their children. Possibly the Scottish equivalent of the English court welfare officer could play – if he does not already – a similarly useful conciliatory role.

In the final analysis it is probably fair to say that the law itself is a blunt instrument for dealing with issues of custody:

> 'The general disposition of the courts against intervention and in favour of maintaining the *status quo* in both contested and uncontested cases is perhaps indicative of judicial realisation of the limited effect that legal proceedings can have in these complex emotional and social conditions' [17].

c) Children in Local Authority Care

In Scotland there are a number of avenues by which children may come into the care of a local authority. Three may be described as compulsory: place of safety orders made under s.37 of the Social Work (Scotland) Act 1968 – hereinafter referred to as 'the 1968 Act'; matrimonial care orders made under s.10(1) of the Matrimonial Proceedings (Children) Act 1958; and care brought about by children's hearings imposing supervision requirements under Part III of the 1968 Act. However, the most common way for a child to come into care is through the 'voluntary' route provided by s.15(1) of the 1968 Act whose importance is such that it is helpful to quote from it at length. It lays down that

> (a) 'it shall be the duty of the local authority to receive a child (under 17) into their care' if it appears that the child is lost or abandoned etc.; or
>
> (b) 'that his parent... is, for the time being or permanently, prevented by reason of illness or mental disorder or bodily disease or infirmity or other incapacity or any other circumstances from providing for his proper accommodation, maintenance and upbringing; and
>
> (c)'... that the intervention of the local authority is necessary in the interests of the welfare of the child.'

The practical importance of s.15, which allows local authorities to give help to families in emergency situations without the need to invoke any formal court procedures, can be deduced from a perusal of statistics for 1983 which show that of the 2,758 children admitted to care that year (not including

Strathclyde Region), 50 per cent were voluntary, 33 per cent were by virtue of children's hearings' non-residential supervision requirements, and 4 per cent were via residential supervision requirements[29].

Regardless of whether care is voluntary or compulsory, it is an area raising important legal, social policy and social work issues. The House of Commons Social Services Committee appreciated this well when they said[30]:

> 'The state has an overriding responsibility to protect children and ensure satisfaction of their basic needs if those caring for them are failing to do so. In the exercise of that responsibility, the greatest caution has to be exercised. State intervention is a last resort. The state can never be substitute for real parents. But when it is necessary, our communal responsibility to protect children must outweigh everything.'

The quotation is instructive in a number of respects not least in its counsel that other measures should be considered before care is used, and that the state is generally only a second best parent. But also underlying the quotation are ideas about two important but possibly conflicting principles. Firstly, the principle that parents are generally speaking the best persons to bring up their children, so that the state should tend to refrain from intervening with the autonomy of the family. The second principle is the importance of the child's welfare which the state has an interest and duty in protecting. Such protection may require interference with the parents' rights to decide how they bring up their children. These two conflicting principles can probably never be totally reconciled, but it is possible for society to work out the balance that these principles should properly strike. Indeed at any one time our system of family law is but a measure of the balance that has been struck. Eekelaar put it well (in a slightly different context)[28] when he said:

> 'The balance struck between them reflects a political judgement about the nature we want our society to have.'

While lawyers are not uninterested in considering the social policies behind the rules governing admission of children into local authority care, they are more concerned with examining the content of the rules, the legal procedures which must be complied with, the legal consequences of being in care, and the 'checks and balances' which operate to protect the interests of all the parties concerned. With these comments behind him, the writer would make the following comments which relate to s.15 voluntary care only.

Section 15 only allows the local authority to 'receive' the child into their care; it does not permit the local authority to 'take' a child into care if the parents object, in which situation the authority would have to use compulsory procedures, e.g. a children's hearing. Once in care the authority have important duties towards their charge, in particular under s.20(1), 'a local authority shall, in reaching any decision relating to the child, give first consideration to the need to safeguard and promote the welfare of the child throughout its childhood.' Here it should be noted that the child's welfare is only the 'first consideration' and not as in custody cases the 'first and paramount consideration'. Furthermore, the duty here applies to any decision relating to the child, e.g. access to parents, whether parental rights should be assumed, etc. Section 15(2) places another duty on the local authority by stating:

> 'Subject to the provisions of this Part of the Act it shall be their duty to keep the child in their care so long as the welfare of the child appears to them to require it and the child has not attained... [18].

This duty might appear to be saying that a local authority could keep a child in the face of a parental request for its return; but at least in the case where care has not exceeded six months this is not so, because the proviso to s.15(3) comes into play which essentially places a duty on the local authority to seek the rehabilitation of the child with his parents, and gives the parents a right to reclaim their child.

> 'Nothing in this section shall authorise a local authority to keep a child in their care under this section if any parent... desires to take over the child, and the local authority shall, in all cases where it appears to them consistent with the welfare of the child so to do, endeavour to secure that the care of the child is taken over by (a) a parent, ...'

On the basis of judicial interpretation [2] these provisions mean that where the parent, even if 'unmeritorious', wishes to recover the child, the local authority cannot keep it on the basis of s.15 [1]. The authority would have to rely on an alternative provisiom, e.g. by passing a parental rights resolution under s.16. If the child has been in care for more than six months, then under s.15(3A) a parent commits an offence if he takes the child away, unless he has given 28 days notice to the authority of his intention to do so or the authority consents thereto. The 28-day period is a 'breathing space' which allows the authority time to consider its plans for the child.

Generally speaking, voluntary care has no effect on the parents' legal rights and duties towards the child [13]. There is possibly some theoretical doubt in the law whether a local authority has the right to restrict parental access, because strictly speaking the parent has not been divested of his right thereto. On the other hand the local authority is under the duty in s.20 to promote the welfare of the child. Regardless of what the strict law is, the practice is now to be seen in the light of the Code of Practice on Access [8]. Applicable to all children in care it enjoins local authorities to put a high priority on maintaining close links between the child and his parents, and to aim at returning children to their families as soon as possible.

3. SPECIFIC LEGISLATIVE DUTIES UPON SOCIAL WORK DEPARTMENTS TO FAMILIES

The list below is not intended to be exhaustive of the statutory duties owed by local authorities (and ultimately social work departments) to individual families but it does contain brief summaries of the more important ones. English local authorities, particularly through the Child Care Act 1980, have similar duties placed upon them.

a) The duty under s.12(1) of the 1968 Act to promote social welfare by giving 'advice, guidance and assistance' on a scale appropriate to their area. The authority is empowered to give 'assistance' in kind and, in exceptional circumstances, cash: s.12(2).

b) To provide home help and laundry facilities for a person in need: s.14.

c) To receive children into care under s.15, which subject has already been discussed.

d) To provide after-care in the form of advice, guidance and assistance to children over school age who were formerly in care: s.26.

e) To secure the welfare of foster children: s.3 of the Foster Children (Scotland) Act 1984, which consolidates all the relevant statutory law on fostering and which gives authorities powers to enable them to discharge their 'welfare' obligations to children.

f) The duty to establish and maintain adoption services: s.1 of the Adoption (Scotland) Act 1978. Under this legislation generally, adoption agencies are charged with specific duties, e.g. to promote the child's welfare as the 'first consideration' (s.6), to regularly visit 'protected' children (s.33), to provide counselling services for adopted children enquiring about their origins (s.45(6)).

g) Under the Mental Health (Scotland) Act 1984 local authorities have a number of obligations: to provide after-care services for the mentally disordered (s.8(1)); to provide suitable training and occupation for the mentally handicapped (s.11); to employ a sufficient number of mental health officers, who carry out important duties in respect of being appointed guardians to the mentally disordered and making applications to the court for the compulsory admission of patients (part V of the Act); and lastly, the duty of the authority to protect the property of the mentally disordered by seeking the appointment of a *curator ad bonis* when no other person has arranged such an appointment (s.92(1)).

4. A FAMILY COURT FOR SCOTLAND?

In a number of countries like New Zealand and Australia, and in certain parts of Canada and the United States, there is to be found an institution called the Family Court. Generally speaking it has exclusive jurisdiction in all aspects of matrimonial law and thus takes in cases involving divorce, custody and access to children, maintenance, adoption and, importantly, juvenile crime. It is a single unified court structure usually made up of two or three tiers, with decisions of courts in the first tier being appealable to a higher-tier court. The personnel who make up the Court are normally legally qualified judges who specialise in family law cases and who, in addition to carrying out traditional adjudication duties, may also act as conciliators or mediators, helping litigants to come to agreements on disupted issues like children's custody and access. The Court also tends to have a corps of full time counsellors who are basically 'in court' conciliators; they help attempts at conciliation (and reconciliation) and assist the Court by producing reports when required. 'Conciliation' and 'reconciliation' are used here in the Finer sense [31]:

> 'By "reconciliation" we mean the reuniting of the spouses. By "conciliation" we mean assisting the parties to deal with the consequences of the established breakdown of their marriage... by reaching agreements or giving consents or reducing the area of conflict upon custody, support, access to children, financial provision etc.'

The Family Court system appears to recognise to some extent that the adversary approach to dispute settlement is not overly appropriate to resolving complex questions of family relationships. The Court seems more willing, at least in some cases, to adopt a more inquisitorial posture, with the judge taking a more active part in the fact-finding exercise.

Could Scotland usefully introduce a Family Court along the lines described above? The Finer Report [31] and more recently the Royal Commission on Legal Services [32] did recommend such an introduction, but successive governments have said that because of constraints on public expenditure they could not give priority to enacting such proposals.

In any case it is doubtful whether Scotland does need a fully blown Family Court. Scotland, perhaps unlike England, already has the basis of a Family Court system in the form of the local sheriff court which has jurisdiction to hear almost all types of family dispute[33]. True, it does not hear cases involving offences committed by children but the system of children's hearings is generally regarded as working well, such that little would be gained by bringing hearings under the umbrella of a Family Court. Instead of introducing a Family Court, perhaps what should be attempted is to build on the present sheriff court structure, for example by introducing the concept of 'in-court conciliation' which appears to work well in the New Zealand Family Court system[34] and in Bristol[35]. The 'in-court' conciliation could complement the great strengths of 'out-of-court' conciliation services like the ones established in Bristol[36] and, more recently, in Lothian, 'Scottish Family Conciliation Service (Lothian)'. Indeed this writer would like to see greater support for the setting up of 'out-of-court' conciliation services because, in his view, if disagreements can be resolved at an early stage in the breakdown of the marriage, then the possible bitterness generated by court actions can be reduced, or removed altogether. Going by the success of the Bristol experience, conciliation shows much promise for the future in helping parties readjust to the effects of family breakdown. Let us hope that promise is realised in Scotland as well.

References

1. Beagley v Beagley *Scots Law Times*. 1984, 202-209.
2. Lewisham London Borough Council v Lewisham Juvenile Court Justices (1979) 2 *All England Reports*. 297-322.
3. Paterson, A. & Bates, St.J. *The Legal System of Scotland*. W. Green, Edinburgh, 1983.
4. Zander, M. *Social Workers, Their Clients and the Law*. Sweet and Maxwell, London, 1981.
5. Martin, F. & Murray, K. *The Scottish Juvenile Justice System*. Scottish Academic Press, Edinburgh, 1982.
6. Hoggett, B. *Parents and Children*. Sweet and Maxwell, London, 1981.
7. Cretney, S. *Family Law (Teach Yourself Books)*. Hodder and Stoughton, Sevenoaks, Kent, 1982.
8. Social Work (Scotland) Act 1968 *Code of Practice: access to children in care or under supervision in Scotland*. Scottish Office, Edinburgh, 1983.
9. Scottish Law Commission *Report on Illegitimacy*. H.M.S.O., Edinburgh, 1984.
10. Law Reform (Parent and Child)(Scotland) Bill, 1985.

11. Clive, E.M. *Husband and Wife*. W. Green, Edinburgh, 1982.

12. Bennett, S.A. *A Short Guide to Divorce in the Sheriff Court*. W. Green, Edinburgh 1984.

13. Clive, E.M. 'Getting Children Out of Dangerous Homes' *Scots Law Times* (News) 1976, 201-208.

14. Clive, E.M. 'Refusing to Return Children to Dangerous Homes' *Scots Law Times* (News). 1976, 265-270.

15. Crighton, A. & Doran, F. 'In Care!' *SCOLAG*. 1978, 4-8.

16. Schaffer, M. 'The Rights of Children and Parents when Children Come into Care' *SCOLAG*. 1985, 72-75.

17. Clarke Hall & Morrison's *Law Relating to Children and Young Persons*. Butterworth, London, 1985.

18. Cretney, S.M. *Family Law*. Sweet and Maxwell, London, 1984.

19. Bromley, P. *Family Law*. Butterworth, London, 1981.

20. Wilson, W.A. 'Divorce for Abracadabra' *Scots Law Times* (News). 1976, 27-28.

21. *Registrar General for Scotland Annual Report 1983*. H.M.S.O., Edinburgh, 1984.

22. Eekelaar, J. & Clive, E.M. *Custody after Divorce*. SSRC Centre for Socio-Legal Studies, Oxford, 1977.

23. *Civil Judicial Statistics 1982*. Cmnd. 9235, H.M.S.O., Edinburgh, 1984.

24. Divorce Jurisdiction, Court Fees and Legal Aid (Scotland) Act 1983.

25. Scottish Office Central Research Unit Papers *The Simplified Divorce Procedure*. Edinburgh, 1984.

26. Scottish Office Central Research Unit Papers *Children in Divorce – A Study of Information Available to the Scottish Courts on Children Involved in Divorce Actions*. Edinburgh, 1984.

27. Eekelaar, J. 'Children in Divorce: Some Further Data' *Oxford Journal of Legal Studies*. 1982, 63.

28. Eekelaar, J. *Family Law and Social Policy*. Weidenfeld and Nicolson, London, 1984.

29. Social Work Services Group *Statistical Bulletin: Children in Care or Under Supervision as at 31 March 1983*. Edinburgh, 1984.

30. Social Services Committee Report, Second Report from the Social Services Committee Session 1983-84, *Children in Care*. House of Commons 360-I, H.M.S.O., London, 1984.

31. *Finer Report*. H.M.S.O., London, 1974.

32. *Royal Commission on Legal Services in Scotland (The Hughes Report)*. H.M.S.O., Edinburgh, 1980.

33. Wilkinson, A.B. 'One Parent Families' *Scots Law Times* (News). 1975, 17-22.

34. Priestly, J.M. 'Mediation Conferences: The New Zealand Family Court's Alternative to Litigation'. In Eekelaar, J. & Katz, S.N. (Eds.) *The Resolution of Family Conflict*. Butterworths, Toronto, 1984.

35. Parmiter, G.M. 'Bristol In-Court Conciliation Procedure' *Law Society's Gazette*. 25 February 1981, 196-197.

36. Parkinson, L. 'Bristol Courts Family Conciliation Service' *Family Law*. 12, 1982, 13-15.

Family Poverty

Malcolm Wicks

INTRODUCTION

The social arithmetic of modern Britain includes the significant statistic that, during 1982/83, the number of people receiving supplementary benefits reached 4 million for the first time. It is a powerful indicator, though just one from many, that the poverty question is one of the most important on the public agenda. Yet, just at a time when more and more families are affected by poverty, the old debate about the concept of poverty (is it a problem that can be measured according to an absolute standard, or is it inevitably a relative concept, and therefore about inequality?) has been rekindled. And this debate is no mere academic one, for it has political and policy significance.

This paper looks at these issues in the following way. It reviews those economic and social trends that have contributed to an increasing number of poor people in Britain. Here the focus is on families with children. Second, it looks at the conceptual question and considers the current debate about the definition of poverty. Finally, and briefly, some of the implications of this for the policy debate are discussed. The paper starts however by briefly setting the current argument in the context of post-war developments.

POST-WAR DEVELOPMENTS

The desire to vanquish 'Want' (or poverty) – one of Beveridge's five giant evils – was at the heart of the Beveridge Reform proposals [1] and was also a major objective of post-war social security legislation.

National Insurance, National Assistance and Family Allowances were key legislative features of the 1940s. Together with the policy objective of full employment, the scene was set for the abolition of poverty as a crucial goal of post-war reconstruction. And for much of the period it seemed as if this goal was well and truly in sight. The 1950s was a period of affluence and economic growth – the so-called 'never had it so good' society in Macmillan's choice words. In the 1950s unemployment seldom rose above 1.5 per cent of the work-force; and in the 1960s it varied between 1.4 per cent and 2.6 per cent. Many British households were visibly enjoying the fruits of increasing affluence in the form of domestic technology and gadgetry; a greater variety of – and more convenient – foods; an increasing range of popular entertainments; cars and foreign holidays.

There was little talk of poverty in the affluent '50s and in the early years of the '60s. Even if poverty was still present among some elderly and disabled people, then certainly it was not felt to be a problem any more for families where the head of the household was in work. Scientific confirmation seemed to come in 1951 when the third survey of York was published. This found that between 1936 and 1950 the proportion of working class people living in poverty had been reduced from 31 per cent to less than 3 per cent (according to the definition adopted) [2]. A *Times* leader hailed this as a 'remarkable improvement, no less than the virtual abolition of the sheerest want' [3]. This supposed 'virtual abolition' of poverty was assumed to be due to the changed circumstances of the post-war period: full employment, an expanding economy, and the impact of the welfare state. This view was strong even within the Labour Party and the 1964 Manifesto spoke only of 'pockets of poverty' [4].

The complacency about poverty was shaken by the work of a number of social scientists in the early to mid-60s. The 'rediscovery' of poverty followed studies by Dorothy Wedderburn, Brian Abel-Smith, Peter Townsend and other researchers, many of whom were associated with Richard Titmuss at the London School of Economics [5].

The 1965 report, 'The Poor and the Poorest', by Abel-Smith and Townsend, was particularly influential and its finding that, 'of all the persons in the low expenditure households as many as 34.6 per cent were in households whose head was in full time work' [6], shattered the myth that full time employment alone was enough to prevent poverty. During the years that followed further research evidence contributed to the re-emergence of poverty as a key social problem, and campaigners, like CPAG's Frank Field, fought to push poverty back into the centre stage of British politics; indeed at the 1970 General Election, CPAG claimed, controversially, that 'the poor had got poorer under Labour' [7]. By the late 1970s, family poverty was even more firmly established on the political agenda and by the early 1980s a number of social and economic trends combined to increase substantially the numbers affected.

SOCIAL AND ECONOMIC TRENDS

There are now several major trends at work which are together increasing the numbers of people who are vulnerable. These trends include unemployment; low pay; and marital breakdown and divorce, leading to growing numbers of one-parent families.

Unemployment

William Beveridge argued in 1942 that idleness, by which he meant unemployment, was

> 'the largest and fiercest of the five giants and the most important to attack. If the giant Idleness can be destroyed all the other aims of reconstruction come within reach. If not, they are out of reach in any serious sense and their formal achievement is futile' [8].

The truth of this statement is now only too apparent in the Britain of the 1980s. Between 1979 and 1983 the unemployment rate increased from 5.3 per cent to 12.9 per cent and the numbers unemployed had increased from 1.3 million to well over 3 million, with non-government estimates putting it much higher [9]. A series of reports from concerned organisations were documenting the impact of unemployment on health, education and other matters. The impact on living standards is, of course, immediate and clear cut. Yet it needs to be emphasised that, while unemployment figures are conventionally expressed in terms of the number of *individuals* out of work, a much larger number of family members are affected.

How many families with children are affected by unemployment? Unemployed heads of households with dependent children fell as a proportion of all unemployed heads between 1976 and 1982 from 61 per cent to 52 per cent. However, the heads of large families were over-represented amongst the unemployed compared to their share of the employed labour force: 12 per cent of the former and 8.1 per cent of the latter [10]. The number of children affected by unemployment has grown significantly in recent years, although up-to-date official data do not exist. However, it was estimated in May 1983 that some 1.2 million children had fathers who were out of work [11]. And figures for 1981 show the impact on family income of a married man with dependent children being unemployed: 82 per cent of such families had income at or below the supplementary benefits (SB) level [12].

Long term unemployment is particularly disturbing. In April 1985 some 40 per cent of the unemployed had been out of work for over one year; and 14 per cent (458,000 individuals) for over three years. This latter group is increasing in number rapidly – by 37 per cent in the 12 months to April 1985 [13].

The Working Poor

The number of poor working families is increasing, as detailed in Table 1 below. In 1979 710,000 families, where the head was in full-time work, had incomes below 140 per cent of the SB level. By 1981 this had risen to 1,130,000 families – 3,840,000 people in all. Eighty-five per cent of these families were married couples with children, and a further 4 per cent were single persons with children.

TABLE 1

Low incomes among working families in Great Britain

	1979		1981	
	Families	People	Families	People
Families with income (thousands)				
Below supplementary benefit level	190	480	240	680
At or above supplementary benefit level but within 20 per cent of it	170	630	310	1,070
Between 20 per cent and 40 per cent above supplementary benefit level	350	1,310	590	2,090
Total with incomes below 140 per cent of supplementary benefit level	710	2,420	1,140	3,840

	1979		1981	
	Families	People	Families	People
Analysis by family type (percentages)				
Married couple with children	68	87	67	85
Single person with children	1	1	4	4
Married couple without children	10	6	9	5
Single person without children	21	6	20	6

Source: *Social Trends 15*, H.M.S.O., 1984, Table 5.16

Marital Breakdown and Divorce

Divorce has also increased the vulnerability of many families to poverty. An estimated one in three of new marriages is likely to end in divorce and the total number of divorces in the UK has increased from 80,000 in 1971 to 162,000 in 1983[14]. Each year a large number of children are affected by their parents' divorce. In 1981, for example, 60 per cent of couples divorcing had children and, of these, one quarter were under the age of five[14]. This phenomenon increases family poverty, and it is one reason why growing numbers of women and children are in poverty.

One-Parent Families

The proportion of families with dependent children headed by a lone parent increased from just over 8 per cent in 1971/73 to over 12 per cent in 1980/82. And while there were an estimated 570,000 one-parent families in 1971, the National Council for One Parent Families now estimates that about 1 million one-parent families exist in the United Kingdom including over 1.6 million children[15]. For all too many, one-parent family status is strongly associated with poverty and deprivation. In 1981 nearly half of all one-parent families were 'poor', i.e. with an income of 120 per cent of SB, compared with one in eight of two-parent families with dependent children[16]. The reasons for this are apparent from an analysis of sources of income, shown in the table below:

TABLE 2

One and two-parent families by main source of income
Great Britain, 1979 (thousands)

	State benefits	Earnings	Maintenance	Other items	Total no. of families with head under pension age
One-parent families headed by a woman	360	330	(50)	(10)	740
One-parent families headed by a man	(30)	70	–	–	100
Two-parent families	270	5,960	–	(30)	6,260

Source: House of Commons Hansard, *Written Answers*, 24 June 1982, cols. 175 and 176.

In 1979 only some 48 per cent of all lone parents had earnings as their major income source, compared with 95 per cent of all two-parent families. However, within the one-parent group those families headed by a man were more likely to have earnings as their main source of income.

NUMBERS IN POVERTY

The numbers of people in poverty can be measured in different ways, but an obvious starting point is the receipt of supplementary benefits. The numbers receiving these have increased from 2.9 million in 1979/80 to 4.3 million in 1984/85. Certainly for families with children means-tested benefits, both supplementary benefit and family income supplement are becoming increasingly important. Indeed, as a percentage of all children in the UK, children dependent on one or other of these means-tested benefits increased from 7 per cent of the total in 1974 to 17 per cent by 1982[17].

This paper has looked at a number of different factors that have contributed to an increasing number of poor families in recent years. Unfortunately, very recent evidence about the numbers affected is not available, but in Table 3 estimates of the number of low income families with children are given for both 1979 and 1981. This adopts as a measure the supplementary benefit scale rate plus 40 per cent. The table shows that between 1979 and 1981 the number of families on low incomes increased from 1.3 million to 1.7 million, and that the number of children affected grew in number from almost 2.4 million to over 3.6 million. This meant that in 1981 nearly one in four families with children were in or on the margins of poverty. This substantial increase is related to another feature of contemporary poverty in Britain. This is, to quote the Government's review of social security, 'the shift over time in the composition of the low income population from pensioners to non-pensioners'. Thus, while in 1971, pensioners made up 52 per cent of the bottom quantile of income units, they represented just 27 per cent by 1982. By contrast, working-age couples with children, where the head of the household was not working, had grown from 5 per cent to 12 per cent of the group during these years [18].

TABLE 3

Low income families with children
Great Britain, 1979 and 1981 (thousands)

	1979	1981
Number of families:		
One parent	430	520
Two parents	700	1190
Total	1130	1710
Number of children with:		
One parent	770	940
Two parents	1600	2680
Total	2370	3620

Note: Low income families with children in or on the margins of poverty are those families with a normal weekly income less than 140 per cent of the supplementary benefit scale rate.

Source: Hansard, col. 146, 20 July 1982; col. 503, 14 December 1983; 'Low Income Families', 1981; D.H.S.S., October 1983.

THE CONCEPT OF POVERTY

So far in this paper 'poverty' has been discussed without defining it. There is, of course, no shortage of literature and research on this question, but recently it has become particularly controversial. And this is no mere academic debate, but a political one also. Any consensus about concepts evaporated along with the end of the larger consensus about the welfare state itself during the 1970s. Moreover, on definitions hang some critical policy implications.

Conventionally, poverty has been defined in either absolute or relative terms; that is it can be measured against an income level adequate 'to obtain the minimum necessaries for the maintenance of merely physical efficiency' [19], to quote Rowntree in his first York study of 1899, or it can be calculated in terms of standards of living more widely experienced within a society. As Townsend explains:

> 'People's needs, even for food, are conditioned by the society in which they live and to which they belong, and just as needs differ in different societies, so they differ in different periods of the evolution of single societies' [20].

It is difficult, however, to translate this relative approach into a workable definition and for this reason a 'poverty line' is often determined in relation to the official supplementary benefit standard. This standard is supposed to provide, in the words of the 1977 Supplementary Benefits Handbook, 'an amount for people to meet all ordinary living expenses' [21]. However, this standard itself has no rational foundation, let alone one based firmly in empirical research. As Piachaud states:

> 'These scale rates are the result of a process of historical evolution with upratings reflecting the prevailing Government's view on the adequacy of the rates, on the relative levels of requirements of children of different ages and for adults, on other claims for public spending, and on wider economic and political circumstances. Broadly speaking the scale rates for children have risen in line with general living standards, reflecting a recognition of the relative nature of poverty' [22].

For some 20 years now, dating from Abel-Smith and Townsend's *The Poor and the Poorest* [6], it has been customary to take the supplementary benefit level plus 20 or 40 per cent as the poverty standard. This has been done on the grounds that, in practice, many benefit recipients receive discretionary weekly additions (for heating, for example) or have certain parts of their income disregarded. Many such claimants therefore have more money than merely the level determined by the supplementary benefit scale rates plus housing costs. Following these research precedents, the official statistics on low income families give one measure in terms of supplementary benefits plus 40 per cent, as is detailed in Table 3.

This convention has, however, come under recent critical scrutiny. Ashton has argued that this kind of measure is quite arbitrary and bears no relation to reality or empirical fact[23]. He notes that the Supplementary Benefit Commission's data for 1976 showed that 88 per cent of SB claimants had an income of less than 110 per cent of the basic rates. For this and other reasons he argues that:

> 'There is no case today, nor has there ever been, for setting the poverty line higher than the State's standard, simply because some beneficiaries enjoy a standard of living above it.'

This scepticism about certain academic definitions of poverty has been echoed by the Prime Minister herself. She has said that there is

> 'No Government definition of poverty... there are many other different definitions of poverty... many of the low-paid on supplementary benefit have incomes about 40 per cent above that level. They are wholly artificial definitions. The fact remains that people who are living in need are fully and properly provided for'[24].

Increasingly the New Right has challenged the definition of poverty, with its implied support for egalitarian measures of social reform. Sir Keith Joseph, in particular, has argued forcefully in favour of an *absolute* standard:

> 'It is not right to turn a discussion of real needs into a discussion of something else by so defining poverty as to introduce into it the very different concept of inequality'[25].

HOW MUCH IS ENOUGH?

Other studies of life on supplementary benefits also show evidence of difficulty. Marshall's study, for example, in 1972, showed that among unemployed men 51 per cent of their children had second-hand shoes; 33 per cent of the mothers had bought their last winter coat six winters ago or more; and 19 per cent of mothers had bought their last new pair of shoes two years ago or more[26]. Debt was another feature of life on SB: a study by the Child Poverty Action Group and the Family Service Units of 65 families revealed that all but one had debts. The debts were generally largest in larger families, and very few families were managing to save anything at all from their weekly benefit to repay them27. Other evidence shows that, among unemployed men with families, 56 per cent had borrowed money for food; 35 per cent for clothing or shoes; and 34 per cent for heating and fuel[28]. These and other studies are analysed in a recent review of research on the adequacy of supplementary benefit. Kenneth Cooke and Sally Baldwin concluded that:

> 'Despite improvements in the real value of supplementary benefit, considerable differences remain between the incomes and consumption pattern of claimants and those of even the poorest families in work. While some claimants appear to manage, many others clearly find it difficult to meet basic day to day needs.
>
> These results do not provide conclusive proof of adequacy or inadequacy. Findings on the appropriateness of the children's rates are however more clear cut. The requirements of children, particularly older children, are almost certainly underestimated in supplementary benefit.'

In practice, while research studies and statistical information are crucial if the debate about adequacy is to be well informed, the poverty question relates to some fundamental value judgements. There will be divisions of opinion, reflecting broader political and ideological differences between those who feel that the poor have reasonable, or at least adequate, benefit provision, in a country that has its own economic difficulties, and those who believe that benefits received by the poor are, in the words of the official Supplementary Benefits Commission in 1978, 'barely adequate to meet their needs at a level that is consistent with normal participation in the life of the relatively wealthy society in which they live' [29].

THE POLITICS AND POLICIES OF POVERTY

What are the implications of contemporary family poverty for social policy? This is not the place for a detailed assessment, but two general conclusions can be drawn.

The first is that trends since the 1940s have undermined the Keynes/Beveridge assumption that poverty would wither away in post-war Britain. Most importantly, 'Idleness' – mass unemployment – has returned with a vengeance and has increased the social security statistics. Beveridge's warning, quoted earlier, that unemployment was 'the largest and the fiercest' of the Five Giants, and that its abolition was crucial to post-war objectives, is one which has a chilling significance four decades after its utterance.

Social change too has played a part. The reforms of the 1940s did not anticipate divorce on the scale that is now experienced, or the consequence of a growing number of families headed by just one parent. Beveridge did, however, appreciate the importance of divorce for social security and he argued the case for this to become an insurable risk. Yet his advice was not followed by the government of the day. In the changed circumstances of the 1980s many people, particularly women and their children, are caught in a financial no man's land between society's willingness to legislate for easier divorce and its reluctance to think through the implications of that decision for policy – social security and taxation policy certainly, but also employment and child-care.

The second conclusion to draw is about the politics of poverty. As shown, there has been increasing and renewed controversy about the concept of poverty, 'renewed' because current debate echoes one with a long history – back to 1834 and earlier. Yet today the stakes are high, particularly for a government that wishes to reduce public expenditure at a time when economic policies are associated with unemployment on a scale that seriously strains the social security system.

If the problem of poverty is relatively small scale, and if those on benefits are provided for adequately, then poverty presents no challenge to social and economic strategy. It can be tackled, or at least ameliorated, by incremental, relatively inexpensive, measures, such as the proposed Family Credit for poor working families. Conversely, if poverty is regarded as a mass phenomenon, and if current benefit recipients are seen to be 'doing badly', then that changes the debate and the policy implications.

Fifty years on from the 1930s – the decade that convinced a generation of politicians, policy makers and reformers (and much public opinion too) that a welfare state was essential – the debate about welfare is at a crucial stage.

References

1. The Beveridge Report. *Social Insurance and Allied Services*. Cmnd 6404, H.M.S.O., London, 1942.
2. Rowntree, B.S. & Lavers, S.R. *Poverty and the Welfare State*. Longman Green, London, 1951.
3. Quoted in Coates, K. & Silburn, R. *Poverty: The Forgotten Englishman*. Penguin, Harmondsworth, 1970, 14.
4. Labour Party. *Let's Go With Labour for the New Britain*. 1964.
5. See Bull, D. (Ed.) *Family Poverty*. Duckworth, London, 1979, Chapter 1.
6. Abel-Smith, B. & Townsend, P. *The Poor and the Poorest*. Bell, London, 1965.
7. 'An Incomes Policy for Families' 1970. Reprinted in Field, F. *Poverty and Politics*. Heinemann, London, 1982, Chapter 7.

8. Beveridge, W. *The Pillars of Security*. George Allen & Unwin, London, 1942, 43.

9. *Social Trends 15*. H.M.S.O., London, 1984, Table 4.18.

10. *Social Trends 14*. H.M.S.O., London, 1983, Table 13.4 & p.185.

11. Hansard, 27 October 1983, Col. 169.

12. *Social Trends 14*. op. cit., Table 13.7.

13. Manpower Services Commission, Annual Report, 1985.

14. *Social Trends 15*. H.M.S.O., London, 1984, Table 13.7.

15. Popay, J., Rimmer, L. & Rossiter, C. *One Parent Families*. Study Commission on the Family, 1983.

16. 'One Parent Families', Fact Sheet. Family Policy Studies Centre, 1984.

17. Family Finances Fact Sheet. Family Policy Studies Centre, 1984.

18. Reform of Social Security, Background Papers, Cmnd. 9519, H.M.S.O., London, 1985, p.10 and Table 1.2.

19. Rowntree, B.S. *Poverty: A Study of Town Life*. Macmillan, London, 1902, 86.

20. Townsend, P. *Poverty in the United Kingdom*. Penguin, Harmondsworth, 1979.

21. D.H.S.S. Supplementary Benefits Handbook. H.M.S.O., London, 1977, para. 43.

22. Piachaud, D. 'The Cost of a Child', Child Poverty Action Group, 1979, op. cit, p.4 (e).

23. 'Poverty and its Beholders' *New Society*. 18 October 1984.

24. Hansard, 22 December 1983, quoted in Mack, J. & Lansley, S. *Poor Britain*. George Allen & Unwin, London, 1985.

25. Joseph, Keith & Sumption, J. *Equality*. John Murray, 1979, 78.

26. Marshall, R. *Families Receiving Supplementary Benefit*. H.M.S.O., 1972.

27. Burghes, L. *Living from Hand to Mouth*. Child Poverty Action Group, 1980.

28. Cooke, K. & Baldwin, S. 'How Much is Enough?' Family Policy Studies Centre, 1984, Table 4.7.

29. Supplementary Benefits Commission. Evidence to the Royal Commission on the Distribution of Income and Wealth. Report No.6: Low Incomes. Cmnd. 7175, H.M.S.O., London, 1978, 28.

Part 2: Practice

The Problem Family Revisited

Marion Lowe and Laurence Tasker

This chapter looks at the notion of the 'problem family' and asks the question, 'Why do social work practitioners continue to label some families as "problem families"?'

While the term 'problem family' may be used as a 'shorthand' by social work agencies, its use is not helpful to the development of good social work practice. It is not helpful for a number of reasons. Typically, the term is used without a working definition, even in some studies having pretensions to serious research. It is thus hard to evaluate the usefulness of methods of intervention dependent on this concept. Further, it has a stigmatising effect in professional usage, probably because it carries with it the hint of consumers taking more than their 'fair share' of resources or through becoming a long-term and immoveable entry on the books of agencies. The label also suggests an assumption of hopelessness in the mind of the labeller – once a 'problem family' label has been put on a case, expectations of positive change may be low. The severity of deprivation confronting members of the family requires a high input of social services resources, but the labelled 'problem family' may receive a minimal input on the basis that 'good money' should not be thrown after 'bad'.

Despite the widespread use of the phrase in social work circles, the expression 'problem family' defies definition by any conventional means of sociological analysis. It is difficult enough trying to come to a common understanding of the nature of the supposedly normal, unproblematic family. As J. Bernandes notes [1]:

> 'Family situations in contemporary society are so varied and diverse that it simply makes no sociological sense to speak of a single ideal-type model of "the Family" at all.'

It would seem that 'the family' itself is a problem in concept to contemporary sociologists. This being so, we may be on a hiding to nothing in trying to seek clarification of the concept of the 'problem family' as distinguished from a notionally normal or non-problem family.

THE IMPRECISION OF SOCIAL WORK'S PROFESSIONAL LANGUAGE

Wide is the literature on the subject of the 'problem family' and Philp & Timms[2], Powell[3] and Miller & Cook[4] all offer useful reviews. The 'problem families' of research studies are characterised by their wide range of interacting material and emotional problems and the presence of dependent children in the care of one or both parents. Some or all of the following factors are usually present: inadequate income, unemployment, bad housing, poor physical and mental health, marital discord, neglect and abuse of children. There may be a period of some years, during which time the family is not seen to have improved in its quality of life, before the family on a social worker's case-load ceases to be a 'family with problems' and becomes a 'problem family'. Once the label has been applied, however, it is a very difficult one to 'unstick' and assumptions about the nature of the family's difficulties may be based on prejudices associated with that label which colour the future social work intervention.

Clearly 'problem family' is a phrase which has come to be used both by social science investigators trying to understand patterns of family life, and by social workers directly involved with clients they have identified as belonging to 'problem families'. But like many a phrase which has been adopted into social work language, it has come to be used widely and persistently while its users neglect or avoid coming to any precise working definition. Just as beauty is in the eye of the beholder, so the 'problem family' exists in the mind of the labeller. We simply do not know, much of the time, whether social worker A's families have any traits in common with social worker B's: the only characteristic they may share is the description put on them.

Indeed, conceptual confusion in the literature on 'problem families' inhibits rather than helps the development of a cumulative body of knowledge on the effectiveness of alternative methods of social work intervention. If we cannot be certain that the 'problem families' worked with so successfully using 'method x' are comparable in the nature of their situation with families with whom we are dealing, how can we generalise the applicability of 'method x' to our work? As Rutter and Madge[5] note:

> 'To a considerable extent, the findings of different studies (and the differences between investigations) are simply a function of how the groups have been defined, and therefore warrant little serious attention.'

The problem of the fuzziness of the 'problem family' and the consequent lack of clarity about what we are talking about, is further compounded by the use of a number of other phrases which are often, though not always, synonymous, such as 'multi-problem family', 'disorganised family', 'family with multiple problems', 'socially deprived family', 'families at risk' and 'severely disadvantaged family'. Such labels tend to promote the assumption that there can be identified a group of families who differ in the nature of their functioning from families in the general population. Given the popularity of the 'problem family' and similar phrases with practitioners, it is important to review how the term has come into use, the evidence to support the existence of the 'problem family' and the function the label plays in policy formation and in determining agency practice.

THE CONCEPT'S HISTORY

One way of understanding the currency of the term is by reviewing its genesis in the social work literature and, in particular, features of its recent usage.

Lahiff suggests that the term 'problem family' began to be used 'about forty years ago to describe those families whose children were particularly neglected and who had multiple and complex problems' [6]. He then sees the term being introduced round about the Second World War and Jordan [7] argues that the phrase caught on in the post war years: 'In the 1950s also the phenomenon of the "problem family" began to be noticed and remarked upon. The post-war services were designed for individual needs, but some families seemed to require several services simultaneously.' Characteristically, such families were involved with the Children's, Welfare and Health Departments, lived in poverty and suffered environmental, educational and cultural deprivation.

Rutter and Madge [5] trace the origins of the concept of the 'problem family' much further back to Booth's epic survey of London's 'submerged tenth', carried out between 1891 and 1903, *Life and Labour of the People in London*. And if we leap on in time to the years of the Second World War, we can see a direct link between Booth's concern with social conditions in the industrial city, and anxiety engendered by the large scale evacuation of city children to families in rural areas during the war years. A report by the Women's Group on Public Welfare, written in 1943, makes reference both to Booth's notion of the 'submerged tenth' and 'problem families':

> 'Within this group (of the submerged tenth) are the problem families, always on the edge of pauperism and crime ... in and out of Courts for child neglect, a menace to the community of which the gravity is out of all proportion to their numbers' [8].

Here we have the fears and fantasies of the relatively affluent in society about the poor: a threat is posed to the wider society by a small group who appear to defy the generally accepted social and moral codes.

The Pacifist Service Units set up during the Second World War to work with the very families who give rise to anxiety amongst the Women's Group on Public Welfare, were much involved in the popularisation of the 'problem family' label. The Units, later to change their name to the Family Service Units, offered intensive casework services to families in some of the larger cities who were suffering from personal and social problems. Stephens [9] noted of the recipients of the Units' help:

> '...each problem family presents a unique complex of circumstances when regarded in its entirety. Innate and environmental factors are inextricably blended though in different proportions in each case.'

While both personality and environment were seen by Stephens to play a part in the production of the 'problem family' the exact balance of the two elements apparently varied. In 1949 the then Secretary of FSU observed:

> 'Generally, both environmental or material factors and personal factors are present; and factors from both these classes converge to bring about the conditions in these families' [10].

What is not clear is where the lines are drawn, if they are drawn, between 'ordinary families' without problems, families having problems in the management of their lives but not to such a degree as to be labelled 'problem families', and families with such difficulties as to justify the 'problem family' classification. If no such lines can be drawn, then we must ask how useful it is to promote the notion of the 'problem family' which acts to confirm a difference between groups which cannot be shown through objective measurement to exist.

Throughout the 1950s the phrase 'problem family' was in common use and articles on the 'problem family' appear in the social work literature. Blacker edited an influential study in 1952 [11] which gave mental subnormality, temperamental instability, ineducability, a squalid home and the presence of numerous children as five commonly recognised features of 'problem families'. The following year Irvine, a psychiatric social worker, published 'Research into Problem Families: Theoretical Questions arising from Dr. Blacker's Investigations' [12], which looked at 'characteristic pathological symptoms both in the individual and in the family group'. Again, the fastidious observer would be concerned that certain families are defined as 'problem families' because of the existence of certain factors, and their attributes are then examined as causal to that definition without seeking to identify the existence of such attributes in the wider population.

In Philp's research, carried out between 1952 and 1958, he looked at the characteristics of a series of families accepted by FSU for long term casework, and sought to identify 'some of the major factors which appeared to create difficulties for these families and to consider how these are related to each other' [13]. He groups together areas of difficulty which appeared to affect some or all of the families: situational problems such as inadequate housing, absence of a male head of household; domestic economy including an irregular income, and income at or below a 'minimum need' level, long term support from public funds, significant debt; home care, to include lack of domestic equipment and lack of domestic routine; child care, to cover physical neglect, cruelty and harsh treatment and children in long term public care; health and adjustment of parents and children including trouble with the law; personal relations within the family, among friends and workmates and with the 'formal network'. He found that 34 per cent of families had problems in seven areas and an additional 36 per cent in six areas, so that 70 per cent might 'justifiably be considered "multi-problem" families'. The one common theme Philp identified among the multi-problem families was poor mental health among the parents. This manifested itself in disturbed relationships both inside the family and in their dealings with the outside world. Surprisingly it was suggested as a causal factor, not a consequence of the demands of bringing up a family in such harsh social and economic circumstances. We might in this connection remember Brown et al. [14] demonstrating the high incidence of depression in working class mothers with young children, depression which was probably the result of being tied to the house and consequent social isolation.

However influential Philp's work may have been at the time, it has serious limitations. There was no attempt to 'match' the FSU families against a random group of families from the same communities or from the wider community. What percentage of problem might have been found among the neighbours of these identified 'problem families' if they too had been open to the scrutiny of a social work agency for a number of years? And at what point does the family seeking help from a social services agency move across from being labelled as a family seeking help with one or a number of problems, to becoming a 'problem family'? The simple answer may be 'when they are referred to FSU'. It must be acknowledged that Philp does recognise that the 'problem family' label is easier to use than to define:

> 'One cannot say on the evidence of this series of families or we believe of problem families generally that there is some single characteristic or indeed one or two general traits which they all have in common and which distinguish them from the rest of the population.'

What begins to become clear as one looks through articles on the 'problem family' is that a crucial definitional element, often poorly acknowledged in earlier work, is the involvement of families with a number of social agencies. As Rutter and Madge conclude from their extensive review of the relevant literature[5], 'In practice, problem families are usually selected on the basis of contact with multiple social agencies.' Factors such as social inadequacy and poor parenting skills may be stressed as factors common to 'problem families' but it is the multiple agency contact which is paramount. Ratcliffe's 1958 study[15] notes that it is involvement with a number of agencies which results in some families gaining a 'problem family' label:

> '...there remains a small number of families in the area which are constantly making demands upon the agencies; which appear to drift from one agency to another, seeking help now about this problem, now about that; families which seem to make no progress, despite all that the agencies can do for them. It is the members of this group which come to be known as "problem families".'

Tonge et al.'s more recent study in 1975[16] defined 'problem families' as those in touch with several agencies. Interestingly, when Tonge compared a group of 'problem families' with multiple agency contact with a control group in contact with not more than one agency, it was found that some of the 'problem families' had fewer social problems than the control group! Indeed, there was a marked degree of similarity, not out and out contrast, between the two sets of families. The one factor which did vary between the two was that there were more breadwinners in regular employment in the control group. Such a finding tends to support the notion that economic difficulties may force some families into contact with social agencies so that their problems become 'public' rather than retained within the family. It also suggests that the notion of an easily identifiable group of 'problem families', with difficulties which are qualitatively and quantitatively different from the bulk of working class families raising children in harsh economic conditions, may be false.

Studies which define 'problem families' as those in contact with a number of social welfare agencies find that 'problem families' are poor families. This is hardly surprising for people faced with personal problems who do not have the economic resources to seek help on the private market, are forced to make use of welfare agencies. Thus, the parent who is in poverty may seek financial help from the local Social Services Department when the DHSS Supplementary Benefit 'giro' cheque does not arrive. A comfortably off family may also fall on temporary hard times, but will be able to call on savings, 'plastic money', or concerned relatives to see them through. Both families may be having difficulties, for example in bringing up their young offspring. But only the parent seeking a Section One payment will have to share his or her child-care problems in order to gain what he or she wants from the social worker The relatively affluent parent does not have to reveal his or her difficulties in child-care to resolve financial problems. But the psycho-social problems in both families may be similar. It is the solution, and consequent likelihood of involvement with welfare agencies, which is different. This is a very important point, for studies demonstrating the poverty of the majority of families in frequent and prolonged contact with social workers, are sometimes used to support the notion that economically disadvantaged parents are 'bad' parents. There is scant evidence to support such a proposition. What poor parents are at risk of, however, is being labelled as 'bad' parents and their poverty being seen, not as a consequence of wider political and economic forces, but a consequence of individual or family pathology. Rutter and Madge confirm that:

> 'Virtually all studies of families who have made contact with multiple social agencies show that they tend to be of low socio-economic status. But this seems not to be the case if epidemiological methods (independent of service contact) are used to select families with multiple psychiatric, educational, marital and delinquency problems' [5].

If 'problem families' are defined as those families in contact with a number of social agencies then we must have many thousands of these families in today's Britain. High levels of unemployment have pushed millions of families with dependent children on to state benefits so that families with children are the largest single group in poverty in this country [17]. Whole neighbourhoods are living in conditions of material squalor and the deterioration in physical and mental health consequent on low income, poor diet and low self esteem, must influence the quality of family life and the raising of children. And these families may be forced to use welfare agencies in order to seek help with child-care problems. But the root of the problems in the bulk of such cases will be economic, and not consequent on parental inadequacy.

THE POLITICAL IDEOLOGY OF THE 'PROBLEM FAMILY'

In 1972 Sir Keith Joseph's 'Cycle of Poverty' speech refuelled the debate about whether families could be identified whose personal characteristics mean that they function at a level unacceptable to the wider society[18]. 'Why is it,' Sir Keith asked, 'that in spite of long periods of full employment and relative prosperity and the improvement in community services since the Second World War, deprivation and problems of maladjustment so conspicuously persist?' The question is posed in such a way that he seemed to be suggesting that certain people are unable to take advantage of available services and live life in adequate fashion because of undefined personal characteristics. Sir Keith went on to suggest that where parents were deprived in their own childhood there was a likelihood that their own offspring would also be deprived and become part of a continuing cycle:

> 'It seems perhaps that much deprivation and maladjustment persists from generation to generation through what I have called a "cycle of deprivation". Parents who were themselves deprived in one or more ways in childhood, become in turn the parents of another generation of deprived children.'

As Bill Jordan notes[19], 'It is perfectly proper for Sir Keith Joseph to ask why in an area of prosperity and improved community services some people are still poor. But the question has nothing to do with maladjustment amongst the poorest sector, when only the former is a distinguishing characteristic of this group.'

Sir Keith had indeed set in motion a massive eight-year research programme, sponsored by the Department of Health and Social Security and the Social Science Research Council, which cost three quarters of a million pounds. Despite the fact that the results of the research provided scant evidence for any links between poverty and maladjustment, the very scale of the investigation must have served to confirm in the public mind the dubious link between poverty and personal inadequacy[20]. And the notion of the 'cycle of deprivation' kept the 'problem family' alive. It gave credence to the supposition that certain families could be identified where parental inadequacies resulted in their children being unable to benefit from education and work opportunities, and going on to produce the next generation of deprived families.

The notion of inheritance of 'problem family' characteristics is present in Ratcliffe's 1968 study, 'Personality Factors in the Problem Family'[15]. Ratcliffe believed that 'problem families' lacked emotional and social maturity, with parents unable to respond in a mature fashion to the needs of the children or to the demands of the world outside the home. He saw their problems as being tackled through long term casework, '... the present generation of problem families may make only a short step forward. But even such a step will have its influence on the next generation. It must be a long term project.' There is little evidence to lift this argument above the level of assertion, which thus exposes the ideological rather than the practical nature of this viewpoint. As Jordan [15] notes, evidence for such cross-generational transmission of inadequacy in emotional and social competence is limited. Wright and Lunn's follow-up study of the offspring of 'problem families' [21] found that two-thirds of the children of the families in the survey did not appear to be creating 'problem families' of their own. Coffield et al.'s research [22] showed no inevitable reappearance of problem behaviour in the sons and daughters of the families studied. This participant observation study of four 'multi-problem' families in a Midlands industrial town, came to the conclusion that Holman's diagrammatic representation of Sir Keith's 'cycle of poverty' [23] did not reflect the families they observed:

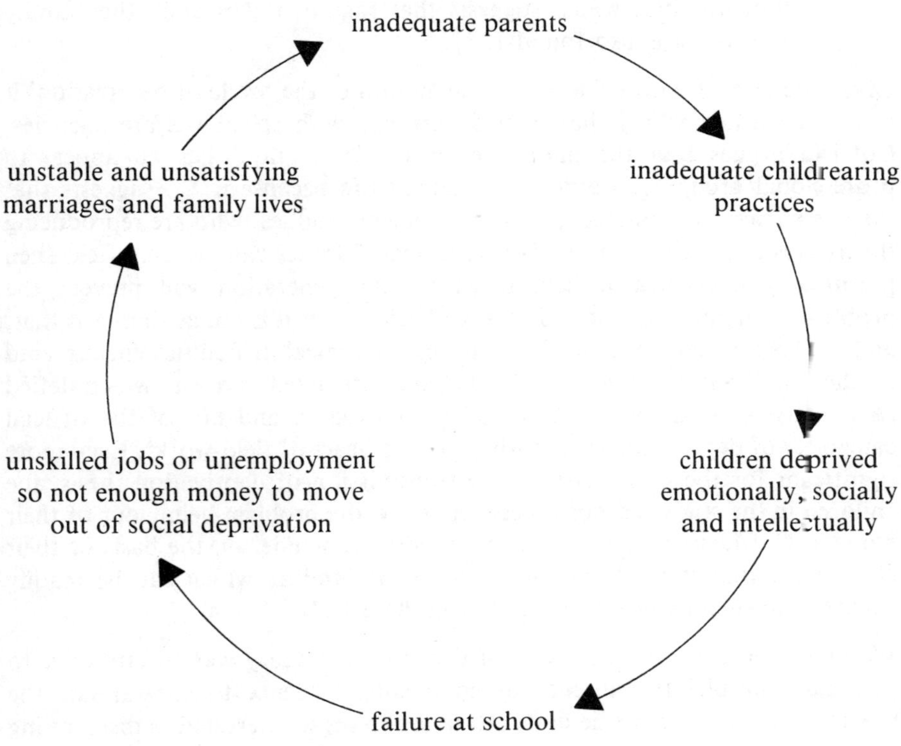

They comment that the idea of 'chain of cause and effect creates the wrong mental image, because it implies a simple, linear progression whereas our data constantly underlined complexity, interaction and contamination amongst variables. No single intervening factor was found (or is likely to be found) to be the transmitter of deprivation.'

Tonge et al. [16] found that there were marked differences between siblings of 'problem families', with some women growing up to provide more than adequate care for their own children, despite a common deprived childhood with siblings who went on to have families who were defined as 'problems'. McLaughlin and Empson [24] found in their research on childrearing styles that the mothers in the study group were not trapped by their own experience of childrearing: they looked to the Health Visitors at the Welfare Clinic, not their mothers for child-care advice. Madge concludes from her exhaustive review of the research inspired by Sir Keith's thesis:

> '... under certain conditions, some family members display consistent patterns. This indicates that like can beget like. At the same time, however, it has provided continuing evidence of widespread discontinuities which suggests that rags to riches and other family contrasts are also found' [25].

Given the lack of hard evidence for the notion of the 'cycle of deprivation' it should be asked why it has gained currency with social welfare agencies. Coffield argues that the phrase 'cycle of deprivation' has an appeal to professional groups concerned with family life because it '... suggests that there is a small containable group of 'problem families' who are reproducing themselves at an alarming rate' [26]. If such families can be identified, then presumably concentrated help given to one generation will prevent the problem recurring in the next. But as Coffield notes, it is not as simple as that, and the social, economic, medical and psychological difficulties encountered by the families in the study overlapped and interacted in a way which defied easy analysis. And the families studied 'moved in and out of the official categories of deprivation even during the two years of field-work'. Even more significant for the trans-generational transmission of deprivation thesis, the children in the study did not necessarily show the problem behaviour of their parents. Coffield's research team were led to conclude, on the basis of their field-work, that 'there is no single group of families which can be readily isolated, labelled as problems, and given help' [22].

We must also ask why the 'cycle of deprivation' theory was so attractive to politicians despite the absence of compelling evidence to substantiate the theory. The answer must lie in its attraction to those interested in dismantling generalised support for family life. Concentration on the supposed personal attributes of a small containable group, apparently incapable of benefiting from commonly available services, deflects attention away from the paucity of support actually provided to the general public. If the problem of the family can be defined, not as the problem many families face of managing the stresses of child-care on an inadequate income (with the mother often having to manage a double burden of paid work outside the home and domestic labour within it), but as a problem of a tiny minority who need additional services not required by the majority, then everything becomes much simpler and much cheaper. And Conservative ideology which promotes the independence of the family and scorns state intervention, can justify intervention in the lives of identified 'problem families' on the basis that additional resources pumped into this generation will prevent costly dependency by deviant families in the next. Overall, normal social functioning is assured by the functioning of the family. Therefore, social malaise is approached on the basis of notional family dysfunction.

THE INDIVIDUAL AND THE FAMILY: IDEOLOGIES AND EXPLANATIONS

It is important that social workers do consider the question of whether specialised services for a few labelled 'multi-problem families', however good, deflects attention from the general paucity of preventative provision for the bulk of clients needing or receiving social work help. For every well-equipped Family Centre, with modern laundry facilities and access to the telephone, how many neighbouring clients have to manage without access to automatic washers, and with a vandalised telephone box down the street? Whatever intervention is utilised to improve the family life of a minority of those in difficulty, the worker must keep in mind the importance of multiple material deprivation in shaping the behaviour of the majority of individuals requiring social work help.

It does not need social work training to realise the effect of material hardship on several fronts on personal social effectiveness. How much more 'poverty research' do we need to acknowledge that, as Rutter and Madge tritely put it, 'Personal burdens and social burdens often interact... It would seem that improvement in social circumstances may be as important for many families as help with their personal problems and interpersonal relationships' [5]. Although such advice might appear unnecessary to those involved in work with families in difficulty, it is remarkable how many social workers do act as if deprived families are totally responsible for the ills they suffer.

A recent article in the *Journal of Family Therapy* offers a good example of the way in which practitioners take for granted the role of psychopathology in creating difficulties in the family, rather than analysing the role of potent external political and economic factors. Craig and Hurry[27] look at 'rural multi-problem families' and give as one of their case studies a family where the husband is a cattleman and he and his wife and six children (and four cats) live in an isolated tied cottage. The home is described as 'dingy, cramped and damp with the roof offering only a scant covering' and is 'unfortunately dilapidated and substandard'. It is noted that 'Trickles of water ran alarmingly close to the two points into which were inserted bare wires from a number of appliances. The two rooms were poorly furnished and dirty with no covering on the cold stone floors.' The house is in the 'middle of nowhere': eight miles from the nearest town, five miles from the village and a mile from the bus stop. In the winter the local roads are often blocked and when the buses are able to run they are infrequent. The couple both suffer from bronchitis, the wife has gynaecological problems and the husband has a foot deformity. One child is enuretic and has a severe squint, another has psoriasis, another epilepsy. Two children attend a school for mentally handicapped children, and one has a severe spinal deformity.

Without knowing the nature of the referral to the therapists, one could guess at the areas likely to present problems to family members. The physical condition of the accommodation is poor; the electric wiring potentially lethal and the dampness and overcrowding must be contributing to ill-health in the family. The physical location of the house, coupled with probable low income and the demands of handicapped children must create huge pressures on the parents. Transport can but be a problem: the family is obviously reliant on an irregular bus service to get the children to school, to go into the village and to do shopping and visit friends. Given that the family apparently have no car they no doubt have to buy food at village store, not supermarket, prices and consequently their food bill will be relatively high.

The ill-health of family members must mean that there are increased demands on the parents, both of whom have health problems themselves. In addition, the mentally handicapped children are likely to bring heavy demands to bear on the parents. The husband's employment – hard physical labour in the open air – is also bound to contribute to the family's problems. We are told that the man works 'long and irregular hours' so that he is likely to be tired when he does get home and not available to share in household and child-care tasks. He is probably lowly paid; agricultural labour is not renowned for high wages and he would not be working long hours if he did not need to supplement his basic wage. The family is in tied accommodation so that the chances are not high that the father will ever be in a position to move into a better-paid job (were it available) because he is trapped by the provision of housing. His wife is likely to be dragged down by the demands of her large family, given her and the family's precarious health, the distance from shops and services and the absence of independent social activities in the vicinity. This is, then, a potential classic 'multi-problem family' suffering from a range of deprivations: substandard housing, poor health, low income, poor access to amenities and services.

The problem this family poses to social agencies, however, is a specific one. It does not directly concern the inadequacy of the material conditions in which they live. Rather, it concerns the father's treatment of his children. This may strike one as reasonable: social work agencies are charged with a statutory duty to ensure that children do receive adequate care and attention within the family. But what if the brutal treatment the father metes out to his children is attributed not to the dehumanising conditions in which he and his family are forced to live – but to his, and his wife's, childhood experiences? This is what happens in this case where the man's excessive punishment of the children 'seemed to reflect the harsh, deprived upbringing that both parents had experienced'. Perhaps this is a contributory factor, but one must be concerned at the way in which this is paid attention to, while the quality of the accommodation afforded the family is simply written off as 'unfortunate' and the heavy demands made on the parents by the poverty of their environment and the family's ill-health is hardly noted.

The parents could be seen as valiant, trying to stay together and raise children in the most difficult of circumstances. How does one achieve satisfactory child-care standards when society does not provide the wherewithal to succeed? How many social workers or child psychologists could cope with six children, living on a low income in the middle of nowhere, without recourse to the birch, or the bottle, or both? What is fascinating is that the worker does actually try to give help with the material difficulties facing the parents, rather than delve into the parents' psychopathology. However, the practical contributions of the worker to improving the conditions in the home are 'excused' as a way of gaining the acceptance of the family to the worker's intervention:

> 'Much time was spent visiting the family at home, engaging with them in ways that were acceptable to them. This often meant giving help with seemingly trivial tasks at a very practical level, for example, mending fuses.'

One must ask who saw the task as trivial; given the comment that the wiring was close to running water one might have said that any activity which contributed to its betterment was far from trivial to the family! And one wonders at the ability of the worker to help the parents maximise their income, and thus be better placed to feed and clothe their children adequately, when it can be stated, '...the family had greeted D.H.'s initial intervention with unceasing hostile abuse, their only apparent interest having been in securing material hand-outs.' It could have been argued more acceptably that the parents were acting responsibly in trying to gain entitlements for their children.

What should one make of professionally trained family caseworkers who see the emotional trees but at the same time seem unable to see the economic and political woods? What faith can one put in the ability of the worker in question to see the world as the family sees it, without prejudice and with some notion of social justice?

SUMMARY

It is worrying that a concept so elusive of precision, or even working definition, as the 'problem family' should gain such currency in professional social work and become the basis of so much agency effort. One might have expected a little more intellectual sharpness for its own sake among professionals who enjoy such extensive periods of further and higher education during training. But it is more serious to contemplate that these workers have embraced a concept which has ideological implications which are more marked than its intellectual or professional appropriateness. The 'problem family' model brings social work closer to Conservative philosophy than to analytical sociology or even conventional casework theory.

At the risk of appearing cynical it might be useful to speculate as to what are the appeals of this approach in current practice. It would be trite to attribute it to any affinity to Conservative values among social workers.

It is pertinent to note the stalemate effect of involving a number of agencies in the management of 'problem families' and the possible advantages of deferring decisions and thus economising on resources once a case has been subsumed under the 'problem family' label. Such consequences must always be of advantage to resource-starved agencies. Moreover, the much inter-worked strands of counselling and resource finding in our profession are richly nurtured in the former respect by a model which depends upon family therapy rather than the mere management of material support. It is sad that a therapy-providing role conventionally has great prestige and apparent job satisfaction accruing to it, compared to the relatively prosaic task of relieving material need.These observations notwithstanding, it is the consequence of this ideology – for thus it is more distinctly than it is a theory – rather than its professional appeal, which must receive our main attention. In particular, we must consider its consequence for the ultimate proper object of practice, namely the needy individual.

If the 'problem family' were to be described thus only in relation to agencies' responsibilities for ensuring 'good enough' parenting, there would be little to quarrel with at the level of general social work usage. Few theorists would wish to abandon the notion of the adequately functioning family as basic to the whole edifice of child-care and related professional concerns. It is its usage in relation to multiple material need evident in one family unit, which makes it theoretically perverse and dangerous in practice.

Any style of explanation in social work which demotes the welfare of an individual relative to that of a community, must be inherently unsound. Undoubtedly, an approach which implies that, notwithstanding the presenting problems of individuals, their solution must be attendant on, and by implication secondary to, a solution to the supposed problem of a collectivity, must be professionally unacceptable. Such is the 'problem family' concept in its inherent tendency to detract attention from the individual needy member. The practice implications of this analysis are no less sinister than the concept would suggest. The individual frequently attracts less agency time and resources and, above all, a diminished sense of agency urgency, once the fateful 'problem family' diagnosis has been applied.

The most worrying feature of the concept, however, is social workers' readiness to embrace the 'problem family' idea in its implied explanation of material need. There is an outrageous manipulation of cause and effect in any version of a problem, of which the above case study is an example, which analyses individual wants as a function of interpersonal processes rather than the other way round. The properly functioning family is an ideal probably achieved only rarely in the most affluent families. To seek it in the family beset by material problems – well documented as a cause of marital disharmony – is to expect saintly rather than mere superhuman qualities of interpersonal skills.

One is reminded of the seminal paper written by John Bennington [28] after lengthy intervention by the Community Development Project in Coventry. It marked a revelation to him that the problems of the Hillfields district would not be relieved by the efforts of CDP, in particular through its 'process' goals. The functioning of a community might, in certain respects, be aided by community work, but the relief of multiple material deprivation would not. It seems time for the death-knell similarly to be sounded over the use of community processes as modes of explanation at that level of 'community' with which we are concerned, namely the family.

References

1. Bernandes, J. 'Do We Really Know What 'The Family' Is?'. In Close, P. & Collins, R.(Eds.) *Family and Economy in Modern Society*. Macmillan, London, 1985, 209.
2. Philp, A.F. & Timms, N. *The Problem of the Problem Family*. Family Service Units, London, 1957.
3. Powell, F. 'Social Work and the Socially Deprived Family'. Unpublished thesis, New University of Ulster, 1979.
4. Miller, J. & Cook, T. *Direct Work with Families*. Bedford Square Press, London, 1981.
5. Rutter, M. & Madge, N. *Cycles of Disadvantage*. Heinemann, London, 1976, 247.
6. Lahiff, M.E. *Hard-to-Help Families*. H.M.& M. Publishers Ltd, 1981, 35.
7. Jordan, B. *Invitation to Social Work*. Martin Robertson, Oxford, 1984.
8. Women's Group on Public Welfare. *Our Towns*. OUP, 1943.
9. Stephens, T. *Problem Families, an Experiment in Social Rehabilitation*. Pacifist Service Units, 1947.
10. *The Development of Family Service Units*. FSU, 1978 (no author given).
11. Blacker, C.P. (Ed.) *Problem Families: Five Enquiries*. Eugenics Society, 1952.
12. Irvine, E. 'Research into Problem Families, Theoretical Questions arising from Dr. Blacker's Investigations' *British Journal of Psychiatric Social Work*. No.9, May 1954.
13. Philp, A.F. *Family Failure: a Study of 129 Families with Multiple Problems*. Faber and Faber, London, 1963.
14. Brown, G.W. & Harris, T. *Social Origins of Depression: A Study of Psychiatric Disorder in Women*. Tavistock Publications, London, 1978.
15. Ratcliffe, T.A. *Personality Factors in 'The Problem Family'*. Institute for the Study and Treatment of Delinquency, 1958.
16. Tonge, W.L., James, D.S. & Hillam, S.M. 'Families without Hope, a Controlled Study of 33 Problem Families' *Brit. J. Psychiat*. Publication No.11, 1975.
17. Social Security Statistics. *Low Income Families, Table 47*. H.M.S.O., London, 1984.
18. Joseph, K. *Speech to the Preschool Playgroups Association*. 29 June 1972, unpublished.
19. Jordan, B. *Poor Parents, Social Policy and the 'Cycle of Deprivation'*. Routledge & Kegan Paul, London, 1974, 8.

20. See Brown, M. & Madge, N. *Despite the Welfare State*. Heinemann, London, 1982; and Fuller, R. & Stevenson, O. *Policies, Programmes and Disadvantage: A Review of the Literature*. Heinemann, London, 1983. Both were published as part of the SSRC/DHSS Studies in Deprivation and Disadvantage inspired by Sir Keith Joseph.

21. Wright, C.H. & Lunn, J.E. 'Sheffield Problem Families, a Follow-up of their Sons and Daughters' *Community Medicine* (London). 126, 1971, 301-307, 315-321.

22. Coffield, F., Robinson, P. and Sarsby, J. *A Cycle of Deprivation? A Case Study of Four Families*. Heinemann, London, 1981.

23. Holman, R. *Poverty, Explanations of Social Deprivation*. Martin Robertson, London, 1978, 117.

24. McLaughlin, A. & Empson, J.E. 'Sisters and their Children: Implications for a Cycle of Deprivation'. In Madge, N. (Ed.) *Families at Risk*. Heinemann, London, 1983.

25. Madge, N. (Ed.) *Families at Risk*. Heinemann, London, 1983.

26. Coffield, F. *Cycles of Deprivation*. Inaugural Lecture, Professor of Education, Durham University, 20 October 1981. University of Durham, 1982.

27. Craig, B. & Hurry, D. 'Rural Multi-problem Families' *Journal of Family Therapy*. 3, 1981, 91-99, Academic Press, London.

28. Bennington, J. 'Strategies for Change at the Local Level: Some Reflections'. In Jones, D. and Mayo, M. (Eds) *Community Work One*. Routledge, London, 1974.

Family Violence: Context and Method

David Gough and Andrew Boddy

Violence within families is not a phenomenon that is easy to understand in ways that suggest straightforward techniques of either preventing its occurrence or modifying behaviour after it has occurred. The provision of services is further complicated by the legal and other social controls that are associated with such violent events. In order to explore some of these complexities it is useful to examine first the different theoretical perspectives that have been applied to this area. This discussion is followed by an analysis of the problem of identification of 'cases' and the context of service provision for one form of family violence: the physical abuse of children. The issues raised then allow for a more general discussion of service provision in family violence, the main emphasis being to show that both social and political standpoints determine practical decisions such as deciding who or what is the client.

CONCEPTUAL APPROACHES

An illuminating way of grouping the different concepts used to understand family violence would be to explore their historical development, but for the purposes of the present chapter it is more appropriate to use a simple classification which considers different approaches according to the level of human or social organisation at which they address the issue. The classification used here has the following five groups: the analysis of general human physiological or behavioural characteristics; studies of individual differences between humans; research on the characteristics of interactions between dyads or within family groups; consideration of aspects of larger groups such as communities or neighbourhoods and, lastly, the relevance of influence of social and political forces. These will be addressed in turn.

General/Biological Characteristics

At the level of individual behaviour, it is possible to study violent behaviour in terms of internal biological states – either as causative or in mediating other causative factors. This level is often used in the study of what is considered to be deviantly aggressive behaviour. Examples are the physiological basis of criminality or violent behaviour [1] or the effects of alcohol and other drugs [2]. It is not common to find formal pathological conditions in the perpetrators of family violence although violence is often associated with high alcohol consumption [3,4]. This may constitute a causative process but many now believe that it is more appropriate to regard it as a correlate of other causative factors such as marital discord [4,5].

There are also theories from psychology and zoology which posit the relevance of basic human characteristics including drives such as aggression. Such theories argue for an innate instinct which has to be dissipated, hopefully in the least harmful way, though Berkowitz [6] takes the view that this optimism is not supported by behavioural work where the use of violence increases rather than decreases the likelihood of further violence. Alternatively, the aggressive behaviour of an individual can be regarded as being modified by the environment and particularly the social behaviour of others [7,8].

Socio-biological explanations have been applied to family violence by Symons [9] and Burgess and Garbarino [10]. An example of their argument is that, if humans have an innate tendency to advance the continuance of their own individual genetic material, then an adult male would be expected to exhibit relative hostility to a step-child, while promoting the interest of his biological offspring.

Individual Differences

Explanations in this area of research are based on theories of personality and development which seek to explain individual differences within both the normal and abnormal ranges. The range of possible theories is immense: they include all personality variables together with individual skills such as impulse control and the ability to cope with stress. This level of enquiry is used not only to understand the peculiarities of the perpetrator; it also attempts to describe victim characteristics such as an unresponsive or handicapped child, or an adult with masochistic needs. This has led to areas of research which are concerned to study both concepts of 'dangerousness' and 'vulnerability'.

Some of the features that have been identified do not belong to the individual but are environmental, such as the stress that may act upon individuals, although the approaches vary in the extent to which they regard this environment as being determined by the individual rather than the other way round [11]. A common suggestion is that of inter-generational transmission, where the experience of physical abuse or the observing of wife battering in childhood leads to the use or acceptance of these behaviours in adult life. In the family violence literature, these approaches are often described as theories of pathology in that they attempt to explain deviant behaviour, but in many cases they do not comprise full theories; they are, instead, a listing of the features that are commonly found in identified perpetrators, victims or environment and so the difficulty is that at least some may well be artefacts of the research methodology. For them to be useful it is also necessary to relate these variables to their occurrence in comparable populations, although such data are commonly lacking. Nonetheless it is an important area of the family violence literature because it is within it that most attempts to devise mechanistic models of causation are located. It is also an approach that is used in devising preventative activities by the creation of schedules to locate risk populations.

Human Interaction and Family Systems

Skills in interacting with other people can be seen as an individual ability but they can also be studied on the basis of the interaction as such. It is possible, for example, to describe a group of individuals who are able to function adequately in some interactions, but have problems in some family situations. Examples in the family violence literature include Kadushin and Martin's [12] study of the interactions preceding violent incidents towards children by parents, and Crittenden's [13] research on how these circumstances may be maintained by the children. Some psychological theories, for example behavioural approaches, have examined the ways that certain patterns of interaction can develop into violence [14]. A more specific example is found in the application of consistency theories where it has been suggested that perpetrators *or* observers may continue to devalue the victim and thus maintain a situation in which violence can occur [15].

The functioning of families as a whole is studied by family therapists [16] and others when differences between families in a range of dimensions, such as power and dominance [17] or adaptability, cohesion and communication [18], are the focus of interest. The therapeutic goal is to change the whole family or family system, although individual or structural change may be a necessary preliminary to this objective.

Communities and Neighbourhoods

This perspective uses several levels of analysis at the same time and so fits somewhere between individual or family analysis and a social or societal approach. In summary, this view argues that violence is likely to occur when those with few internal resources live in a situation of environmental poverty (either material or emotional) and with social norms that are more accepting of violence. The emphasis is on the relevance of the environmental conditions for preventive work. To some extent this approach has similarities with Gelles' [3] early model which used a flow diagram to illustrate the many factors which work at different levels and interact to precipitate child abuse. Many authors have suggested a multi-causal approach, but the importance of the ecological perspective proposed by Garbarino [19] is that it stresses the neighbourhood as the best level for intervening in these problems. The preventive strategy would be to support positively the emotional and material resources of local communities in order to diminish the problem of violent and abusive behaviour within families.

Social and Political Explanations

Social or political approaches explore the social context in which the violence occurs and are often critical of explanations of family violence based on individualistic or pathological models. If violence is regarded as 'the use of force in situations where the community defines the use of force as illegitimate' [12] then the socio-political view is not interested in the deviance of those instances that overstep this line, but in how the line of legitimacy is drawn and enforced. This view concerns itself with aspects of societal norms, social structure and power – for example in the relationships between men and women, parents and children and the family and the state. Within this general perspective, these writers differ from each other in the extent to which they employ a historical and political analysis of the situation. Gelles [20], for example, proposes an 'exchange' or social control model where individual behaviour is determined by different kinds of rewards and costs; Gelles suggests that structural effects, such as the degree of privacy and extent of social controls within families, either raise or lower the level of constraint or inhibition towards family violence. Although this theory may be applied in clinical work with families, it is included here because it primarily addresses the way in which social controls can have consequences for both families and individuals.

More explicit social-political approaches take a broader view of social norms and controls and the way that they are supported by the reactions of, for example, the police and legal system [21] [22] and the health and welfare agencies [21] [23] to family violence. These responses then limit the options that are available to abused individuals so that other political actions may lead to alternative solutions to problems of family violence. The best example is the development of Women's Refuges and the organisational form they have taken [24].

There are, in addition, theoretical critiques of the levels of analysis described earlier which are seen as individualising the problem and thus diverting attention from underlying structural inequalities [25]. Therapy and social responses for individual or family pathology are seen at best as palliative and at worst as reinforcing inequalities particularly when they 'blame the victim' [24] [26] [27]. These criticisms extend to ecological theories of impoverished neighbourhoods because although they argue for social change, their basic premise is that there is some 'fault' in the community [22] – or its members collectively – that requires treatment or correction.

PHYSICAL ABUSE TO CHILDREN

All the theoretical perspectives discussed above can be applied to all the different forms of family violence and have implications for both preventive and reactive solutions. On the other hand, their implications and their utility for practice can only be adequately tested by examining them in the context of reactions to specific forms of family violence. For this reason it is helpful to focus on one area: physical abuse of children has the merit of having the most extensive literature and many of the conclusions to be drawn from this work may apply to other manifestations of the larger problem.

The different definitions of the physical abuse of children come down to the common theme of the experience or risk of an adversity by a child which is to some extent a consequence of an inappropriate environment – usually child-care or parenting environment. Definitions vary in their interpretation of the experiences that they consider adverse and in their attribution of responsibility within the caretaking environment. There are in addition different assumptions about the way the two interact to produce different judgements and cut-off points about what is abusive or what is 'non-accidental'. Theoretical definitions are rarely specific as to where these criteria or cut-off points occur; in practice, they are achieved by the application of theoretical definitions to individual cases although not always in an explicit or consistent fashion.

The Process of Identification

In simple terms, the process of identification starts with an injury in a child, which may then raise questions about the adequacy of parenting and the possibility of the injury being the product of inappropriate force or violence. This process of identification (that is, applying definitions in practice) is a complex process of which we know little, but is of crucial importance for two reasons. Firstly, it is used to decide whether a particular child or family causes concern and warrants the offer of a service including the use of different procedural and legal systems and the possibility of forceful intervention. If, as is often said, the priority is to protect the needs of the child, then we need to know much more about how such decisions are made and the outcomes they provide for the child and the parents. The second reason is that it is the most common method of recruiting research samples and so has the consequence that most research data focus on the characteristics of identified cases without sufficient consideration of the process by which these samples are defined. The effects of this bias on an understanding of the problem will be obvious [28].

It has been shown by two sets of American researchers, Giovanni and Becerra [29] and O'Toole, Turbett and Nalepka [30], that different professional groups vary in their criteria for deciding whether a case is abusive or not. The problem for professional workers is greater than the existence of different criteria for abuse because in practice cases are not like vignettes and 'all the facts' are not known. It is commonly believed that the injuries themselves reveal the story but work by Dingwall, Eekalaar and Murray [31] has found that the suspicion of casualty officers was aroused by their social assessments of the family rather than by distinctive features of the child's injuries.

Although certain injuries can become associated with physical abuse, the clear physical signs represented in child abuse texts do not make up a majority of cases. The concept of abuse usually includes the attribution of responsibility; this requires more than the clinical evidence of an adversity such as physical injury.

A more formal operational definition of physical child abuse is placement on a child abuse register. This is significant because registration usually invokes local child abuse procedures and so defines the child or family as a 'case' for the system. The interest then becomes one of how agencies behave in these circumstances. Bacon and Farquar [32] and Hampton and Newberger [33] have both shown that the criteria for registration are not applied uniformly and that variations are not simply due to the use of different criteria for 'abuse' but also to the considered needs (or effects) of placement on the register.

The behaviour of professional agencies has also been studied by Dingwall et al.[31] who suggest that agencies work on a 'rule of optimism' and prefer to take the least coercive line, although this is less likely if the parents are regarded as being 'incorrigible'. In this way, an isolated incident after extreme stress in the family may be less likely to be registered if the family are then extremely co-operative and accept help. On the other hand, registration may also be less likely if the case conference is concerned about a family's negative reaction and thus the likely consequences for trusting relationships with the agencies. This observation has also been used as an explanation for the low referral rates of cases to social work from general practitioners[34].

At the same time, as Hallett and Stevenson[34] remind us, case conference decisions are the product of complicated intra-group processes being acted out by people with very different professional roles. A summary of research in this area presents a picture of a very complex process that uses social information to identify cases of physical abuse; once identified, families may be offered services within one of the theoretical perspectives or may be 'managed' in ways that constitute a mixture of the ideas that these perspectives propose.

Extent of the Problem

National estimates are produced by examining the number of cases identified by the relevant agencies. There is no central recording system in Britain but the NSPCC maintains the child abuse register for approximately 10 per cent of the child population of England and Wales. For 1982 they found a physical abuse injury rate of 0.63 per 1,000 children under 15 years and they extrapolated these figures to estimate that 6,388 children are physically abused each year in England and Wales, of which 647 are serious or fatal[35]. In America there have been many widely varying estimates; the National Center on Child Abuse and Neglect[36] estimate a physical abuse rate of 3.4 per 1,000 children under 18 years.

It will be clear that there are many problems in attempting to make national estimates of the incidence of a phenomenon when there are both varying theoretical and operational definitions of the phenomenon itself. The range in rates of identification between geographical areas, for example, has varied by a factor of ten within the Glasgow area[37]. A large part of these differences must be due to reporting practices but they go beyond those of variation in formal definition. The NSPCC statistics[38] show a range that is close to a factor of three between three English cities which use the same criteria for registration.

An alternative and more fruitful approach has been to consider violence towards children within families in the general population when corporal punishment appears to be extremely common. John and Elizabeth Newson[39] found that a sample of mothers smacked 75 per cent of their four-year-olds and 41 per cent of their seven-year-olds at least once a week. More worrying is the finding of an American population survey by Straus, Gelles and Steinmetz[40] who reported that 4 per cent of parents had used 'abusive violence' (including kick, bite, punch, hit or try to hit with an object, threat or use of a knife or gun) in the previous year on their three- to 17-year-old children. Another American study by Korsch et al.[41] found that a quarter of 100 mothers interviewed had started 'spanking' their child within the first six months of life.

The extent of physical punishment in 'normal family life' raises many questions of the basis for research and intervention in physical child abuse. In addition to the identification problems discussed earlier, research in this context underlines the problem of estimating incidence rates, of determining whether physical abuse is a growing problem and the difficulty of identifying which are genuine causative processes. Of even greater importance, these observations raise questions about the relationship of abuse to the norms of different social groups and the consequence of labelling different behaviours as deviant.

Intervention in Physical Assault of Children

The discussion to this point has examined several different aspects of the *context* in which services identify and offer a service in child physical abuse, whatever theoretical perspective is taken. The professional agencies still need to decide how to react and may turn to the research literature in order to assess the effects of different forms of intervention. Unfortunately it is unable to provide clear answers.

There is some research which reports high rates of reinjury of abused children[42]. Although the intensive involvement of professionals does seem to reduce this rate, the effect on such measures as the quality of parenting and the cognitive development of the children is less convincing[43,44,45,46,47]. Hensey and Rosenbloom[48] report fewer problems among children who are received quickly and permanently into care but this outcome has to be balanced by literature concerned with the breaking of children's bonds with their psychological parents[49], and the possible long term effects for children in care[50].

In brief, research is unable to provide guidance about which intervention applied within which theoretical perspective would provide a solution either for a particular family or as a more general strategy. This leaves agencies with the problem of how to react in specific situations and of how to ensure that children are sufficiently protected. In its turn, therefore, the social work role cannot avoid at least some degree of social policing which includes a coercive role that can range from the offer of a 'voluntary' service, to the legal loss of powers of the parent. The implications of this conclusion are that difficulties in unravelling the complexities of definition, identification, prevalence and knowledge about the efficacy of interventions must also take questions about individual rights into account. This means balancing a parent's right to bring up their child and a child's right to be brought up by its parent as well as its right to be protected from adverse experiences. Considerations of this kind have five features that are relevant for the social work management of cases of this kind.

The Rights of the Child. Even if there were good information as to the long term consequences of different experiences, there is still a judgement to be made as to the relative rights of a child not to have certain experiences compared to the rights of parents to bring up children in the way that they choose. This is a complex issue that produces much debate and is ultimately value-based and thus political [22,49,51,52]. This can be particularly relevant when one considers the pervasive nature of violence in families found by Straus et al.[40] and the adversities faced by children in certain sub-groups of the population as reported, for example, by Essen and Wedge[53].

Parents' Rights. Parents' rights have also to be taken into account; parents may require a service to enable them to exercise their rights and this will include enabling them to make decisions about their own futures in addition to help with other emotional or material needs.

Balancing Needs. Even if the child's interests are primary and if there were sufficient research knowledge about long term outcomes[54], the reality is that services become involved at times of crisis when assessment is difficult. It may thus be necessary to attempt to resolve the separate needs of parents before it is possible to assess (and maybe achieve) the best options for the child and its long term future in the context of the original family. An unfortunate consequence can be that the emphasis is focussed on changes required in the mother as the most usual primary caretaker of the child.

The Legal Context. All the above forms part of the casework strategy and yet major decisions about a case may be dependent on decisions by courts (and Children's Hearings in Scotland) which are influenced but not determined by recommendations from social work and other agencies. This can mean that the strategy itself is qualified by legal decisions, anticipation of them or the use of legal powers in enforcing an approach to the management of a case.

Coherence of Relationships. All the above takes place while the worker is attempting to develop constructive relationships with the child, the parents, and workers from other agencies. All may have different perceptions and may differ in their willingness to identify with a particular interpretation of the situation and the management strategy that is proposed. An individual worker may thus face confusion in establishing coherent relationships with the whole family and conflicts with other professionals who are also engaged within the family.

POLICY IMPLICATIONS

This broad overview of the context of interventions shows that the decisions of agencies, particularly social work, cannot avoid being judgemental and must involve the taking of risks. Decisions will have consequences but they have to be made without the confidence that they are supported by research and usually with little personal or local feedback as to the likely outcome of the choices that are made. This uncertainty is emphasised by society's ambivalence towards both the use of violence and the relative rights of parents and children. It follows that a coherent basis for social work's involvement in family violence can only be achieved by clarifying the socio-political position. Only then is it possible to decide what is a case, who or what is the client, and what general perspective should be taken in providing a service, and especially, whether this should be preventive or consist of *post hoc* interventions.

In recent years there has been the development of local procedures in order to ensure good practice. These probably have benefits in ensuring that certain vital actions are not overlooked, but many of their requirements are stated in broad terms that do not help workers to make some of these crucial socio-political distinctions. This has the advantage of preventing a too centralised or bureaucratic position on these issues, but it also has the drawback that the procedures may limit the ability of workers to exercise professional judgement without providing anything in its place.

The theoretical perspectives with which this paper began, the deficiencies of the research literature in providing a basis for practice and broader socio-political considerations all combine to suggest three broad conclusions about the present state of our understanding of the physical abuse of children, at least for the provision of service or the development of policy. These are:

The Societal Context. Child physical abuse is distinguished from other difficulties for individuals or families by both the value judgements and knowledge base necessary before intervening in family life. The concentration of attention in the literature on the individual and family characteristics has distracted attention from their social, procedural and legal context. This is not to suggest that the only meaningful level of analysis is the social or political level, but that coherent work at the individual or family level (where services are definitely needed) requires a clearer specification. Only then will there be clarity as to the methods and the purposes of intervention.

The Specificity of Services. The identification of child physical abuse is not a straightforward or 'mechanical' process and is highly problematic. The difficulties that such children and their families experience requires the provision of services, but there is little evidence to suggest that these services should be qualitatively different from other kinds of service apart from the elements of social control. In other words, the intent of therapeutic interventions should be based on assessments of individual and family functioning rather than on the nature of an abusive incident. This is an argument for clarifying the socio-political *context* of services in ways that facilitate the effectiveness of the interventions they are able to undertake.

Procedural Guidelines. Guidelines for procedure, produced by agencies, would be of greater help to their workers if they at least clarified the important judgements that need to be made. These need not be prescriptive, but they should provide help for individuals or case conferences in weighing up the competing aspects of the probability of further violence, the rights of individuals and the social responsibilities of agencies. Developments of this kind might, for example, alter the tendency of case conferences to seek a consensus position in favour of more explicit debate about the different judgements implicit in their overall conclusions about a case. It might thus assist decisions as to the necessity for more than one worker to be involved in a case in order to represent the interests of different clients.

OTHER FORMS OF FAMILY VIOLENCE

The main conclusion to be drawn from our discussion of adult-to-child violence is that none of the five theoretical approaches with which this paper began provides an adequate basis for developing methods of intervention. One reason for this conclusion is simply the lack of research evidence, but it is also important to regard these perspectives as to some degree hierarchical and to appreciate that methods relating to individuals or families also exist within the socio-political level of analysis and the value judgements that are implicit in it. What this means is that practical interventions are an amalgam of two different influences. On the one hand, we can describe the phenomenon of family violence and expect research (however imperfectly) to propose mechanisms of cause and thus solutions or treatments. Simultaneously, however, we must acknowledge that the socio-political interpretation of family violence creates a system of value judgements which determine both the research that is done, the relevance it has to practice, as well as the context and framework in which agency responses occur.

A similar situation exists in regard to other forms of violence within the family. The nature of the violence may be different as may be the social judgements that are made and the agency responses that have evolved. What is shared is a need to clarify the relationships between these three different aspects and this argument is well illustrated by the example of violence between married and cohabiting couples.

There are obvious differences in society's attitudes to violence to children and to adults. One distinction is the dependent nature of the child in the family[24] which makes it more difficult for the child to seek a service – particularly since the parents have authority over the child. In addition, there are specific legal aspects which concern the State's preparedness to intervene in family life in order to protect children. Adult victims may choose to leave a violent home but they are unlikely to be required to do so by the State, nor is it usual for the State to provide protection within the home as it may do for children. Differences of this kind reflect differences in the social context of the two kinds of violence, but this does not imply that their underlying characteristics are essentially different, whether this be causal accounts of individual behaviour or in the underlying socio-political position taken by society.

There are few studies of family violence in the general population but all have found high rates of marital violence. For example, Straus et al.[40] report that 16 per cent of the couples interviewed had used violence in the previous year and 28 per cent had used violence at some point in their marriage. There were not large differences as to whether it was the man or woman who was violent but the male violence was more severe. This is confirmed by studies examining cases identified by agencies. Dobash and Dobash[21] found that the vast majority of cases reported to the police were wife assaults, and Berk et al.[55], using similar American data, found that women were much more likely than men to have received injuries in the incidents of marital violence that were investigated. Retrospective analyses of women who have left violent relationships and moved to Women's Refuges, have shown that the violence was not an isolated incident and that they had made several previous attempts to leave[4].

There has also been research on the experiences these women had of the agencies they approached, and several authors[21] [56] [57] discuss the way that the police, legal and housing systems are organised in a way that minimises effective help particularly in regard to the opportunities that are open to women in difficulties. There are few empirical studies of social work intervention that do not depend on retrospective accounts by clients, but a study by Maynard[23] examined a random sample of social work records and found that in a quarter of the cases (27 out of the 108 casework records) the cohabiting or married woman was reported to have been beaten in the last 12 months, and a third of them over a two-year period. Of these identified cases, two women were immediately admitted to a mental hospital and three were referred to marriage guidance. The impression of the remaining cases was that the social workers may have acknowledged problems in the males but that their advice or support was directed towards how the women should behave in order to minimise the violent behaviour they were experiencing. This is a conclusion that imputes blame or fault on the part of the women, but it needs to be viewed alongside the work of Bowker[58] or Deschner[59] who accept that women may have reasons for remaining within the family and thus concern themselves with ways of minimising violent behaviour.

As with parent-child relationships, violence is a common form of marital interaction and so there are similar problems of identification and of the consequences of taking or not taking certain actions. There are strong pressures on all agencies to adopt a neutral stance in marital conflict but its effect is to put the responsibility for changed behaviour on to the woman. In cases of child abuse, there is, in practice, a very similar outcome because the mother is usually the principal caretaker and is considered responsible for the child's protection. Specific features of practice may vary between the two situations but the basis of both forms of work is again dictated by socio-political judgements and the context in which the service is offered.

CONCLUSION

This paper has reviewed the range of theoretical perspectives used to understand family violence which suggests approaches to prevention and intervention. On examining the broad context of the identification of cases and the context of service provision in the particular area of child physical abuse, it became clear that it was not a simple process of finding and then applying a 'treatment'. The pervasive use of physical force within families and the conflicts of interest between individuals, family and society mean that action or inaction on the part of the agencies must be value-based.

This complexity makes it difficult to propose direct relationships between the results of research and the needs of practitioners and thus to make full use of the theoretical approaches described at the beginning of this chapter. An examination of violence from men to women in families reveals similar problems concerning the context of service provision. It seems that although there may be variations in the specific nature of these problems, they are likely to be basically similar across the whole range of family violence. This paper has not examined this full range but more information can be found in the works of Cloke[60], Gelles and Cornell[61], Kosberg[62], Martin[63] and Russell[64].

Research into family violence can serve two purposes: it can provide knowledge about the causes and mechanisms of the problem and thus propose methods of prevention or intervention; it can also inform the process of intervention by investigating the social or organisational context in which it takes place. We have argued that this second area of activity is necessary for an understanding of the first and that – as an aspect of family violence – it has been relatively neglected. A greater emphasis on this aspect of the problem could have a number of practical benefits. It would make it easier to identify casework objectives and thus allow feedback about the value of particular activities and appropriate assessments of outcomes[65]. It would provide a clearer understanding of the scope and limitations of service provision, with the benefits of showing up gaps in the services provided and reducing the anxiety of workers in cases where the content of tasks is often intangible and responsibilities can seem to be limitless. Finally, it would give workers greater protection when their case management is thought to have gone wrong. With the benefit of hindsight, it is easy to judge decisions as having been wrong simply by shifting the socio-political standpoint from which these judgements are made; this risk is increased if the basis of initial management decisions is not explicit in the first place.

References

1. Hinton, J.W. 'Biological Approaches to Criminality'. In Brain, P.F. & Benton, D. (Eds.) *Multidisciplinary Approaches to Aggressive Research*. Elsevier/North Holland, Amsterdam, 1981.

2. Taylor, S.P. & Leonard, K.E. 'Alcohol and Physical Aggression'. In Geen, R.G. & Donnerstein, E.I. (Eds.) *Aggression, Theoretical and Empirical Reviews*. Academic Press, New York, 1983.

3. Gelles, R.J. *The Violent Home*. Sage, Beverley Hills, 1974.

4. Pahl, J. (Ed.) *Private Violence and Public Policy. The Needs of Battered Women and the Response of the Public Services*. Routledge & Kegan Paul, London, 1985.

5. Gelles, R.J. *Family Violence*. Sage, Beverley Hills, 1979.

6. Berkowitz, L. 'The Goals of Aggression'. In Finkelhor, D., Gelles, R.J., Hotaling, G.T. & Straus, M.A. (Eds.) *The Dark Side of Families*. Sage, Beverley Hills, 1983.

7. Lorenz, K. *On Aggression*. Methuen, London, 1966.

8. Snowdon, C.T. 'Ethology, Comparative Psychology and Animal Behaviour' *Annual Review of Psychology*. 34, 1983, 63-94.

9. Symons, D. *The Evolution of Human Sexuality*. Oxford University Press, Oxford, 1979.

10. Burgess, B.L. & Garbarino, J. 'Doing What Comes Naturally? An Evolutionary Perspective on Child Abuse'. In Finkelhor, D., Gelles, R.J., Hotaling, G.T. & Straus, M.A. (Eds.) *The Dark Side of Families*. Sage, Beverley Hills, 1983.

11. Mischel, W. 'On the Interface of Cognition and Personality. Beyond the Person – Situation Debate' *American Psychologist*. 34, 9, September 1979, 750-754.

12. Kadushin, A. & Martin, J.A. *Child Abuse. An Interactional Event*. Columbia University Press, New York, 1981.

13. Crittenden, P.M. 'Maltreated Infants: Vulnerability and Resilience' *Journal of Child Psychology and Psychiatry*. 26, 1, January 1985, 85-96.

14. Frude, N. (Ed.) *Psychological Approaches to Child Abuse*. Batsford, London, 1980.

15. Wagstaff, G.F. 'Attitudes to Rape: The 'Just World Strikes Again'' *Bulletin of the British Psychological Society*. 35, 1982, 277-279.

16. Bentovim, A. 'Theories of Family Interaction and Techniques of Intervention' *Journal of Family Therapy*. 1, 1979, 321-345.

17. Straus, M.A. 'A General Systems Theory Approach to the Development of a Theory of Violence between Family Members' *Social Science Information*. 12, 1973, 105-125.

18. Olson, D.H. & McCubbin, H.I. *Families – What Makes Them Work*. Sage, Beverley Hills, 1982.

19. Garbarino, J. 'An Ecological Approach to Child Maltreatment'. In Pelton, H. (Ed.) *The Social Context of Child Abuse and Neglect*. Human Sciences Press, New York, 1981.

20. Gelles, R.J. 'An Exchange/Social Control Theory'. In Finkelhor, D., Gelles, R.J., Hotaling, G.T. & Straus, M.A. (Eds.) *The Dark Side of Families*. Sage, Beverley Hills, 1983.

21. Dobash, R.E. & Dobash, R. *Violence Against Wives*. Free Press, New York, 1979.

22. Freeman, M.D.A. 'Freedom and the Welfare State: Child Rearing, Parental Autonomy and State Intervention' *Journal of Social Welfare Law*. 1983, 70-91.

23. Maynard, M. 'The Response of Social Workers to Domestic Violence'. In Pahl, J. (Ed.) *Private Violence and Public Policy. The Needs of Battered Women and the Response of the Public Services*. Routledge & Kegan Paul, London, 1985.

24. Schechter, S. *Women and Male Violence. The Vision and Struggles of the Battered Women's Movement*. Pluto Press, London, 1982.

25. Hanmer, J. & Leonard, D. 'Negotiating the Problem: The D.H.S.S. and Research on Violence in Marriage'. In Bell, C. & Roberts, H. (Eds.) *Social Researching, Politics, Problems, Practice*. Routledge & Kegan Paul, London, 1984.

26. Overfield, K. 'The Packaging of Women: Science and our Sexuality'. In Friedman, S. and Sarah, E. (Eds.) *On the Problem of Men*. The Women's Press, London, 1982.

27. Wardell, L., Gillespie, D.L. & Leffler, A. 'Science and Violence Against Wives'. In Finkelhor, D., Gelles, R.J., Hotaling, G.T. & Straus, M.A. (Eds.) *The Dark Side of Families*. Sage, Beverley Hills, 1983.

28. Boddy, F.A. & Gough, D.A. 'The Causes of Child Abuse – A Sensible Research Question?' Paper presented at D.H.S.S. meeting, 'Research Issues in Child Abuse'. Oxford, November 1982.

29. Giovanni, J.M. & Becerra, R.M. *Defining Child Abuse*. Free Press, New York, 1979.

30. O'Toole, K., Turbett, P. & Nalepka, C. 'Theories, Professional Knowledge and Diagnosis of Child Abuse'. In Finkelhor, D., Gelles, R.J., Hotaling, G.T. & Straus, M.A. (Eds.) *The Dark Side of Families*. Sage, Beverley Hills, 1983.

31. Dingwall, R., Eekalaar, J. & Murray, T. *The Protection of Children. State Intervention and Family Life*. Blackwell, Oxford, 1983.

32. Bacon, R. & Farquar, I. Unpublished paper reported in *B.A.S.P.C.A.N. News*. 13, 1984, 4-6.

33. Hampton, R.L. & Newberger, E.H. 'Child Abuse Incidence and Reporting by Hospital: Significance of Severity, Class and Race' *American Journal of Public Health*. 75, 1, 1985, 5660.

34. Hallett, C. & Stevenson, O. *Child Abuse. Aspects of Interprofessional Co-operation*. George Allen & Unwin, London, 1980.

35. Creighton, S.J. *Trends in Child Abuse*. N.S.P.C.C., London, 1984.

36. Burgdorf, K. *Recognition and Reporting of Child Maltreatment*. Westat, Rockville, 1980.

37. Gough, D.A., Boddy, F.A., Dunning, N. & Stone, F.H. 'Research Problems in Understanding Non Accidental Injury Families'. Paper presented at Congress of the International Association of Child Psychology and Psychiatry, Dublin, July 1982.

38. Creighton, S.J. & Outram, P.J. *Child Victims of Physical Abuse: A Report on the Findings of N.S.P.C.C. Special Unit's Registers*. N.S.P.C.C., London, 1977.

39. Newson, J. & Newson, E. *Seven Years Old in the Home Environment*. George Allen & Unwin, London, 1976.

40. Straus, M.A., Gelles, R.J. & Steinmetz, S.K. *Behind Closed Doors: Violence in the American Family*. Anchor/Doubleday, New York, 1980.

41. Korsch, B., Christian, J., Gozzi, E.K. & Carlson, P.V. 'Infant Care and Punishment: A Pilot Study' *American Journal of Public Health*. 55, 12, 1965, 1880-1888.

42. Rosenbloom, L. & Hensey, O.J. 'Outcome for Children Subject to Non-accidental Injury' *Archives of Disease in Childhood*. 60, 1985, 191-192.

43. Baher, E. et al. *At Risk: An Account of the Work of the Battered Child Research Department, N.S.P.C.C.* Routledge & Kegan Paul, London, 1985.

44. Berkeley Planning Associates. *Evaluation: National Demonstration Program in Child Abuse and Neglect*. Berkeley, 1977.

45. Lynch, M.A. & Roberts, J. *Consequences of Child Abuse*. Academic Press, London, 1982.

46. Martin, H., Beezley, P. 'Therapy for Abused Parents: Its Effects on the Child'. In Martin, H.P. (Ed.) *The Abused Child: A Multidisciplinary Approach to Developmental Issues and Treatment*. Balinger, Cambridge, 1976.

47. Oates, R.K., Peacock, A. & Forrest, D. 'The Development of Abused Children' *Developmental Medicine and Child Neurology*. 26, 5, 1984, 149-156.

48. Hensey, O.J., Williams, J.K. & Rosenbloom, L. 'Intervention in Child Abuse: Experience in Liverpool' *Developmental Medicine and Child Neurology*. 25, 5, 1983, 606-611.

49. Goldstein, J., Freud, A. & Solnit, A.J. *Beyond the Best Interests of the Child*. Free Press, New York, 1973.

50. Quinton, D. & Rutter, M. 'Parenting Behaviour of Mothers Raised 'In Care''. In Nicol, A.R. (Ed.) *Longitudinal Studies in Child Psychology and Psychiatry. Practical Lessons from Research Experience*. Wiley, Chichester, 1985.

51. Dingwall, R. & Eekalaar, J. 'Rethinking Child Protection'. In Freeman, M.D.A. (Ed.) *State, Law and the Family. Critical Perspectives*. Tavistock, London, 1984.

52. Parton, N. *The Politics of Child Abuse*. MacMillan, Basingstoke, 1985.

53. Essen, J. & Wedge, P. *Continuities in Childhood Disadvantage*. Heinemann, London, 1982.

54. Clarke, A.D.B. & Clarke, A.M. 'Constancy and Change in the Growth of Human Characteristics' *Journal of Child Psychology and Psychiatry*. 25, 2, 1984, 191-210.

55. Berk, R.A., Berk, S.F., Loseke, D.R. & Rauma, D. 'Mutual Contact and other Family Violence Myths'. In Finkelhor, D., Gelles, R.J., Hotaling, G.T. & Straus, M.A. (Eds.) *The Dark Side of Families*. Sage, Beverley Hills, 1983.

56. Freeman, M.D.A. 'Legal Ideologies, Patriarchal Precedents and Domestic Violence'. In Freeman, M.D.A. (Ed.) *State, Law, and the Family Critical Perspectives*. Tavistock, London, 1984.

57. Brynn, M. 'Domestic Violence: a Question of Housing' *Journal of Social Welfare Law*. 1984, 195-207.

58. Bowker, L.H. *Beating Wife Beating*. Lexington Books, Lexington, 1983.

59. Deschner, J.P. *The Hitting Habit. Anger Control for Battering Couples*. Free Press, New York, 1984.

60. Cloke, C. *Old Age Abuse in the Domestic Setting – A Review*. Age Concern, 1983.

61. Gelles, R.J. & Cornell, C.P. *Intimate Violence in Families*. Sage, Beverley Hills, 1985.

62. Kosberg, J.I. (Ed.) *Abuse and Maltreatment of the Elderly, Causes and Interventions*. John Wright, Bristol, 1983.

63. Martin, J.P. (Ed.) *Violence and the Family*. Wiley, Chichester, 1978.

64. Russell, D.E.H. *Sexual Exploitation. Rape, Child Sexual Abuse and Workplace Harassment*. Sage, Beverley Hills, 1984.

65. Sheldon, B. 'Group Controlled Experiments in the Evaluation of Social Work Services' *Research Highlights No.8: Evaluation*. University of Aberdeen, Department of Social Work, Aberdeen, March 1984.

Loss: Bereavement, Illness, and Other Factors

Hugh Jenkins

INTRODUCTION

This chapter aims to highlight some of the salient factors associated with loss in the family. Loss is dealt with both in a specific sense in relation to death, and as a general, more pervasive theme. In doing so, a certain degree of depth in any single area has had to be sacrificed. I am taking the same view in this respect as Finkelhor [1] does when considering violence and the family. He points out the large number of specialisms which have grown up, each focussing on a particular area of abuse. Often this is linked to requirements for obtaining research money. The effect of this, he suggests, is to miss some of the common features associated with violence, in the search for discrete differences. It is also important to remember that loss, however defined, always takes place in a context of place and time. This will frequently be in the context of family or a significant social group, and loss will always have an effect on someone beyond the individual. For the sake of convenience, loss here is described in terms of 'the family'. A therapeutic parallel is that the therapist always intervenes in the family, for to see an individual is to make a choice about intervening in a 'family' [2], even if the family is not physically present.

DEFINITION OF LOSS

My working definition of loss is: the disappearance of a significant object or attribute which has high physical, emotional or psychological survival value for the individual(s) concerned. This is the person's subjective experience of the loss, since loss of a particular object or attribute for one person may have a different value for another. The relative effect(s) of loss will be mediated by time and circumstance.

This broad definition allows us to consider a wide spectrum of human experience, which includes: loss through death, including stillbirth, abortion and miscarriage; illness, whether acute or chronic, and whether physical and/or psychiatric; handicap, both physical and mental; divorce or separation; in terms of separation this can be extended to include loss through normative life cycle processes such as adolescence and leaving home; further normative life cycle loss may include loss of faculties to cope associated with ageing. Loss may be the result of external factors over which the individual has little or no control, such as unemployment, 'natural' disaster, or accident. In the area of psychological loss, I would include loss of trust through the experience (especially in children) of incest or physical abuse, and associated trauma. An instance of this would be the psychological abandonment experienced by a daughter for her mother's failure to protect her from the sexual advances of a father. This list is not definitive. Clearly, there is a danger in seeing every aspect of human difficulty as linked in some way to loss. Yet it may prove to be a more useful generic concept than, for example, considering many problems associated with the 'adolescent' phase of 15 years to 30 as a 'leaving home problem' [3,4]. After all, the problem of leaving and letting go is ultimately also one of loss and of losing. It is hoped that this exploration will be useful in the application of ideas for the development of practice in social work.

LOSS THROUGH DEATH

Death clearly represents loss, both for the person who is dying, and for those left behind. The data adduced in this section are applicable in other areas of human experience outlined later in the chapter when considering loss in a much broader form. Research studies and implications for practice go together in this process.

Murray Parkes [5] writes:

> 'Of all the functional mental disorders almost the only one whose cause is known, whose symptomatology is stereotyped and whose outcome is usually predictable is grief. That grief is a mental disorder there can be no doubt, since it is associated with all the discomfort and loss of function which characterise such disorders.'

It may sound almost contradictory to describe a normal, expectable process as disordered. However, loss through the death of someone will create psychological, emotional, and even psychiatric impairment for a period. It may further result in physical impairment as a concomitant of the other aspects. It is because grief can lead to dysfunction that it is morbid or pathological [6]. Parkes attempts to 'systematise the various types of reaction which follow a major bereavement'. His paper highlights the atypical responses to bereavement as manifested in a group of psychiatric patients. The range of symptoms is not in itself dysfunctional, but the important aspect to emerge for the individual grief sufferer is one of extended duration. In none of the sample was the grief briefer than in the normal population, that is, a population not requiring psychiatric treatment. Parkes does point out one difficulty in his study, in that: 'It has not always been possible to determine if a particular feature exhibited by the patients studied here is a part of the usual reaction to bereavement or a morbid form of it.'

In his companion paper, Parkes [7] considers the classification of bereavement reactions, making the point that bereavement is a common stress, and only a small proportion of those who suffer it are referred for professional help. He subdivides bereavement reactions into (1) the stress-specific grief response and its variants, and (2) non-specific responses. These two subdivisions are further divided:

(a) The stress-specific reactions – grief and its variants:

(1) Typical grief
(2) Chronic grief
(3) Inhibited grief
(4) Delayed grief.

(b) The non-specific mixed reactions. Any of the above along with:

(1) Psychosomatic reactions
(2) Psychoneurotic reactions
(3) Affective disorders not resembling grief
(4) Other conditions.

Space prohibits a lengthy analysis of this paper and the subclassifications. However, Parkes [7] describes typical grief as characterised by:

> 'the onset, after a brief period of numbness, of attacks of yearning and anxiety alternating with longer periods of depression and despair. The sufferer is preoccupied with thoughts of the dead person who is commonly felt to be present. These features, along with the associated symptoms of insomnia, anorexia, irritability and social withdrawal,

soon begin to decline in intensity, although they may return from time to time at anniversaries or other reminders of the loss.'

Although relatively early papers, these are useful in setting the scene for understanding grief and loss. The study that Parkes conducted was of loss by death of a first-order relative. However, the literature indicates that loss of a home[8] or the loss of a limb[9] result in similar processes.

Before turning to more recent work on bereavement, it is worth reviewing the seminal paper by Lindemann[10] on aspects of acute grief. The four major points made in this paper are:

1. Acute grief is a definite syndrome with psychological and somatic symptomatology.
2. This syndrome may appear immediately after a crisis; it may be delayed; it may be exaggerated or apparently absent.
3. In place of the typical syndrome there may appear distorted pictures, each of which represents one special aspect of the grief syndrome.
4. By appropriate techniques these distorted pictures can be successfully transformed into a normal grief reaction with resolution.

The courses of normal and morbid grief reactions are compared. In the latter, two major categories of delayed reactions and distorted reactions are identified, with nine separate possible subdivisions for distorted reactions that may be described as morbid. They are: over-activity without a sense of loss; acquisition of symptoms belonging to the last illness of the deceased; a recognised medical disease; alteration in relationship to friends and relatives; furious hostility against specific persons; repression of hostile feelings resulting in conduct resembling schizophrenia pictures; lasting loss of patterns of social interaction; activities detrimental to the bereft's social and economic existence; and, a reaction which takes the form of agitated depression, where the individual may be dangerously suicidal. One of the important observations from this paper, which arises from the study of 101 patients some of whom were bereaved disaster victims (the Cocoanut Grove Fire), is that the relative intensity of relationship, whether positively or negatively so, with the deceased before death was significant. Lindemann observes:

'Not infrequently the person who passed away represented a key person in a social system, his death being followed by disintegration of the social system and by a profound alteration of the living and social conditions for the bereaved. In such cases readjustment presents a severe task quite apart from the reaction to the loss incurred. All these factors seem to be more important than a tendency to react with neurotic symptoms in previous life.'

Although formal psychiatric prognostic formulation is usually based partly on pre-morbid characteristics, Lindemann suggests that in the instance of acute grief this may not be such a prominent pre-disposing factor as the quality and social significance of the severed relationship. Parkes [7] also points out that the age of the deceased will have an effect on the relative impact. Thus the death of a very elderly person will be experienced as part of the natural course of events whereas the death of an adult in his middle years or of a child will not. The responses of an adult to death will also differ from those of a child11. These findings are important for professional practice decision-making, their relevance being brought home all the more acutely by the recent (1985) football disaster in Bradford with the loss by fire of some 56 people of all ages.

In their chapter on 'Acute Reactions to Stress', Garmezy and Rutter [12] survey childhood reactions to stress across a broad range of situations. They describe briefly the effects on children of the Buffalo Creek Flood where 125 people lost their lives [13]. One of the significant related factors for children who suffered psychosocial impairment was the degree of parental impairment and this is similar to Lindemann's conclusions. (The findings in relation to children in this study are taken from a sample population of 230 children aged less than 16 years, almost equally divided in numbers between the two sexes.)

Birtchnell has conducted a series of studies examining some of the psychiatric effects of parent death. He affirms that there is a difference between the death of one parent where the other survives, and the death of the second parent. The death of the second parent is often more traumatic and may represent a finality which cuts links in a different way than when a surviving parent remains. The loss of both parents together, or of the second parent, also propels the child into a different generational relationship for himself, and for his own children, if any [14]. In his study examining the relationship between mental illness and early parent death, Birtchnell [15] looked at a group of 482 psychiatric patients and a control group of 476. The study is interesting because it shows that while there is little difference overall between patients and controls, taking age of subject as between 0 to 19 at time of parent death (29.9 per cent compared to 24.3 per cent), the differences become increasingly significant until in the 0 to 4 age range, the difference is that 9.8 per cent of patients lost a parent whereas only 4.7 per cent of controls did. Birtchnell proposes that it is important to look at the incidence of early parent death in detail if one is to find any significant relationship between loss and subsequent mental illness in later life. There may be a loading related to high parental age at time of parent death. However, he says:

> '... there is little difference between the mean parental ages at birth for patients and controls who have suffered early parent death... This would indicate that the raised incidence of early parent death in the patients is a primary phenomenon and is not secondary to increased parental age at birth.'

Further on in his discussion, Birtchnell concludes that:

> '... the eventual effect of early parent death is that from the time of death onwards, the child must survive without that parent though there may be a substitute parent. This finding supports the view that it is not so much the trauma of separation from the parents as the continued absence of the parent throughout childhood which is the important aspect of early parent death.'

In a companion paper, Birtchnell [16] discusses his findings relating early and recent parent death to the incidence of depression. The psychoanalytic field has always paid attention to object loss, especially that of the mother, as an important formative factor in psychological development. (A useful introduction to a psychoanalytic perspective is provided by Malan [17].) Birtchnell uses the same subjects as in his first paper [15] and shows that 'there is a relationship between the incidence of both early and recent parent death and the severity of depression', and: 'In young subjects, the recency of the event, rather than the fact that it occurred in early life, is the important aspect of the parent death.' This is not surprising since such an event may be less expected, but a significant difference remains which suggests that young patients (aged less than 40) are more sensitive to recent parent death.*

Finally, the work of George Brown should be mentioned [18]. In this study on depression and loss, Brown and his co-workers identify the significance of loss before age 11 years as significant in terms of future mental health. He distinguishes between psychotic patients as more likely to have had a past loss than neurotic patients, that is 66 per cent as opposed to 39 per cent. A distinction he makes is that:

> '... within the psychotic group (of patients) severity of symptoms is

*In his current work, Birtchnell is coming to the view that it may not be the loss itself which has long-lasting effects, but that it is the effects of the (familial) reorganisation following loss and the problematic relationships which constitute the pernicious or detrimental factors. His view now is that the loss *per se* does not necessarily have the long term effects that the psychoanalytic field proposes.

> highly related to loss by death and within the neurotic group to other forms of loss.'

This study is too complex to report in detail, but it does appear that environmental factors are of as great if not greater importance to the effects of loss than constitutional or genetic factors. Rather than viewing depression solely as a noxious factor, it may be as Brown suggests, that there is a protective function:

> '... it has been suggested that many of the depressive symptoms which the patient forms may be regarded as helping him to *avoid* experiencing painful loss, and in particular helping to deny the fact of loss and the significance of the loss.'

and:

> 'It is possible that loss by death may be related to psychotic-like symptoms because it tends to lead to a very general attitude that one's own efforts are useless; that loss of any kind becomes like death, irreversible, and there is nothing that can be done.'

These considerations, originating from formal research findings, lead us to questions of practice in relation to loss by death.

DEATH AND PROFESSIONAL HELP

I have considered a number of studies describing the impact of death on the bereft individual. My focus has been on psychiatric disorder and grief, while pointing out that there may be physical or psychosomatic sequelae following bereavement. Much of the traditional therapeutic focus for work with those who have suffered loss by death has been primarily individual (c.f. Malan [17]; Pincus [19]; Parkes [20]). What is clear is how often the effects of earlier losses impinge upon or are reawakened at the time of a more recent bereavement, and also how early losses which remain in some significant way unresolved often affect current relationships. It has been suggested that losses across two or three generations may continue to exert strong adverse influences on the individual. Clearly, it is often useful for the bereft to receive individual help to deal with long-lasting or recent unresolved grief reactions. Psychoanalytic treatment may often uncover a link between distant loss and current difficulty either in terms of subjective personal distress or interpersonal relationships. This is a legitimate area of practice, although frequently one that it is difficult to carry out in a busy social services office. It demands a particular kind of commitment and intensity by the professional and the client. I have had referred clients of this nature from area team colleagues precisely because the direct pressures of under-staffed inner city offices make such work impossible. This should not be an excuse for condoning poor practice, but equally many clients of social services departments would find it difficult to use a formal psychoanalytic or psychodynamic approach to treatment. It is important to note however that it is rare for the effects of bereavement to be felt by only one person. Therefore, I wish to consider some of the work from the more recent family therapy or family systems literature in this connection. Lieberman [21,22], Palazzoli et al. [23] and Paul [24] all consider the importance of involving the family in their clinical work. Lieberman focusses on the trans-generational dimension, and clearly this has links with the psychoanalytic field insofar as the emphasis is upon family history as it affects current functioning. This is an important point in the family therapy literature, where great emphasis is often placed on the here-and-now aspects of current functioning, almost to the exclusion of past events. Minuchin [25] emphasises that history is important, not for itself, but to the extent that the past is alive in the present. Palazzoli and her colleagues have given considerable attention to the importance of family myths as they become part of family life, and they focus interventions around family rituals as a means of rendering past events less dysfunctionally potent in the present [26]. The role of myth in the family has been discussed by Ferreira [27] and Byng-Hall [28]. They partly link a psychoanalytic and systems framework, demonstrating how powerful myths in families shape lives and can be used therapeutically to help change dysfunctional patterns that have evolved around emotive themes. This theme will be returned to later in discussing a paper by Pattison [29]. Paul in his work uses a technique known as 'operational mourning' which forces the patient – individual, couple or family – to face their grief directly [6, 24, 30]. The important aspect of this work is its interactional and interpersonal nature, while also dealing with intrapersonal experience. As Black [31] points out: 'The resistance to doing the work of restructuring is what the pain of grief is about.'

Having mentioned a number of practitioners who have developed approaches in their field, I will outline some more general aspects of death and the family system. Bowlby-West [32] looks at the impact of death in terms of the family in a useful brief paper. She writes:

> 'Clergy, rabbis, bereavement counsellors and all "helping" professionals should be encouraged to see a bereaved person in the perspective of the family system and the family-community system... An essential part of griefwork is tracing old and unfinished mourning

where death in previous generations has had an impact on the present generation.'

Based on the work of Bowlby and Parkes, she also describes the phases of grief.

So far, the emphasis has been on the effects of bereavement on the individual. It is important to remember that each individual in a family will experience grief in his or her own specific way. This means that the relative length of different phases will vary, as will the intensity as mediated by age, experience, and nature of relationship of the bereft to the deceased. The four phases described by Bowlby-West are:

1. A numbness phase that may last from a few hours to a week and may be interrupted by outbursts of extreme anger or distress. Coping with everyday tasks is difficult, due to incomprehension, denial and preoccupation with the loss.

2. A phase of yearning and searching for the lost figure which can last months or, often, years. A period of intense inner struggle in which awareness of the reality of death conflicts with a strong impulse to recover the lost person and the lost family structure.

3. A phase of reorganisation and despair; feelings of hopelessness in which the grieving person is aware of the discrepancy between his inner model of the world and the world which now exists.

4. A phase of greater or lesser degree of reorganisation, development of new sets of assumptions that includes finding a new personal identity.

In a useful paper, Gelcer[33] pursues both the question of phases and differences as affected by the individual's life cycle stage:

> '... it has been found that adults go through clearly delineated stages of mourning, the completion or disruption of which leads respectively either to resolution or complications. Children... are far more limited than adults in their ability to conceptualise death, and this ability varies according to their age or cognitive level. Children's expressions of grief therefore vary accordingly but are also a clear function of the nature of their relationship with the dead, the circumstances of the death, and, in the case of a deceased parent, the sex of the parent and the ability of the surviving parent to provide a supportive environment for successful mourning.'

As Herz[34] points out, in her examination of the inter-relationship of age at death of the deceased, the life cycle stage(s) of the family, and the significance for the family system of the deceased (c.f. also Lindemann[10] and Gleser et al.[13]), the degree of disruption is affected by a variety of factors. The four most significant are:

1. the timing of the death or serious illness in the life cycle,
2. the nature of the death or serious illness,
3. the openness of the family system,
4. the family position of the seriously ill, dying or dead family member.

From a therapeutic standpoint, the only aspect which the professional helper can attempt to affect and change is the degree of openness of the family system. 'Therefore, most family interventions before, at the time of, or after death, are directed toward opening up the family emotional system.'

Families, and individuals, will use homeostatic adjustments to cope with stress[35]. Bowlby-West[32] identifies and describes 12 such homeostatic adjustments in family systems. These are: anniversary reaction; displacement of feelings; enmeshment; family secrets; generation gap; idealisation; infantilisation; obsessive paranoia; pathology; replacement; restructuring – role changes; trans-generational mourning. These are all useful pointers to problems that families may display in grieving. In his study of 'Nineteen Cases of Morbid Grief', Lieberman[6] emphasises the importance of 'understanding... the nature of the normal mourning process, the ability to diagnose the morbid reaction and finally the ability to confront the patient in a way which will unblock the mourning process'. He underlines the importance of family involvement in treatment (as does Gelcer[33]). He concludes from the research carried out in conjunction with his work on 19 cases, admittedly a small sample, that:

> 'Family involvement in the treatment seems to be beneficial, and clinically it was common to discover that morbid grieving was a family pattern so that other members of the family needed to experience the forced mourning as much as the identified patient. Family members, when not included, tended to block the therapy by not allowing emotional expression of anger, grief and loss at home.'

Lieberman's description of 'forced mourning' is equivalent to 'operational mourning' described by Paul[24] and Paul and Paul[30]. Difficulties in grieving after a recent loss may stem from difficulties related to earlier significant losses. Gelcer[33] indicates: '...the problems children have as adults when they have not successfully mourned. These problems include such reactions as depression, difficulties with gender identity, various somatic complaints, and even psychosis.' This is borne out in large part by Brown et al.[18] in their work on depression and loss. The failure to mourn successfully an early loss is dramatically described by Pattison[29] from a psychoanalytic object-relations perspective. (For an analysis of object-relations and attachment theory in family therapy, see Heard[35].) The case study by Pattison is interesting in terms of an individual therapeutic focus which combines with an understanding of family systems. Pattison discusses his work in the context of his five basis theses:

1. much of the observed psychopathology of experiences with death during childhood results from a socio-cultural failure to integrate death appropriately as part of natural life experience;
2. the family system incorporates and embodies this cultural denial of death;
3. the family management of death is dysfunctional for both the family and the child because it fails to integrate death appropriately within the family;
4. the family deals with death through the avoidance mechanisms of family myth and family mystification;
5. the family myth and mystification processes are the pathogenic elements in the death of a family member rather than the death *per se*.

The case described and the discussion certainly support these hypotheses.

Pattison[29] emphasises the dangers of not being able to mourn a loss, especially if the individual never knew the lost object in the first instance. It is important to emphasise the adaptive nature of the mourning process, which has psychological, and in the case described by Pattison, physical survival value, just as attachment behaviour in the very young has high survival value. In her chapter, Black[31] puts in perspective the painful processes of mourning. She writes:

> '... under the impact of reality-testing, when loud calling and crying does not bring him back, the realisation of loss impinges, and protest gives way to despair. The features of this stage of grief are identical to a depressive illness except that we know the cause. The features of depression which are adaptive are the repetitious rumination and the

> withdrawal which aids the restructuring of one's internal assumptive world. Those people who avoid the depression of bereavement by ceaseless activity indeed "come to grief" later on in both senses of the phrase.'

The important lesson to be drawn from this, as from the research studies and case studies described earlier, is that if adequate mourning fails to take place, either naturally, or facilitated by voluntary workers or professional helpers, then both short and long term problems can be psychiatrically and physically incapacitating [31,36].

The act of mourning can be particularly difficult when there is nothing to mourn, as in the case of stillbirth. This event is too often one that professionals and family members deal with as a non-event; the pregnancy that never was, since no live being comes at the end of the gestation period. The fact that there never was a possibility to establish a human relationship with a stillbirth heightens the importance of grieving, since: 'Like other dead children, stillbirths are idealised; this accentuates the ambivalence and needs to be understood' [37]. The particular problems in grieving the loss of that which never had a chance to be are discussed in Lewis38, Lewis and Page [37] and Meyer and Lewis [39]. Similar considerations apply in work where there has been an abortion.

What is clear is that work with the bereaved is stressful. It should not be lightly undertaken, or without adequate colleague support. Parkes [20] considers some of the implications for this, and maintains that:

> '... professional services and professionally supported voluntary and self-help services are capable of reducing the risk of psychiatric and psychosomatic disorders resulting from bereavement. Services are not beneficial among bereaved people who perceive their families as unsupportive or who, for other reasons, are thought to be at special risk... The value of services that lack the support of trained and experienced members of the care-giving professions remains to be established.'

In concluding this paper, he points out that bereavement by death is not the only kind of loss which professionals are called upon to deal with, and some aspects of the wider field will now be considered.

LOSS THROUGH ILLNESS

It is relatively simple to chart the major issues related to the effects of loss through death. Failure to mourn adequately is likely to lead to disturbance of functioning at one or more levels: physical, psychological, psychiatric or emotional. Symptoms may be experienced as acutely real, yet without obvious organic cause. Illness, whether chronic or acute, can result in loss of individual capacity to function, and will affect the family or social context within which it happens. Grolnick [40] reviews the literature on psychosomatic illness from a family perspective. As discussed earlier in this chapter, bereavement may result in illness of some kind which will represent a loss of functioning in relation to the original loss or losses. There is a higher incidence in individuals of illness and disability following bereavement. When faced with illness, it is always worth asking about recent or early losses. However, illness, unrelated to preceding loss itself may well represent direct or indirect loss. It may represent curtailment of ability to engage in normal activity. It may entail loss of opportunity for other family members through economic hardship, and loss of status for the ill person.

Grolnick's paper is an interesting introduction to the field of psychosomatic illness. He classifies, according to the current literature, into: intrapsychic, dyadic, and familial categories. He says:

> 'Family relationships influence the onset and course of psychosomatic illness and of many organic illnesses. Some family factors are changes in role, membership, and biological status (puberty, marriage, pregnancy, divorce, illness, menopause, senium, and death).'

Illness, as with death, is never truly an isolated event. 'Illness will provide active feedback within the family system. It may stabilise it, resulting in medical attendance patterns of a chronic illness, or feedback may further unsettle things, resulting in psychosomatic outbreaks or other dysfunction in other members.' [40]. An important aspect about illness, whether physical or psychosomatic, is that it may be the result of the stress associated with loss; it may result in loss, as discussed above; or it may encompass both. Finally, illness or incapacity in one family member may well have a protective function for another member. By this I mean, for example, that a wife's depression may help the husband to feel competent in a coping or caring role, whereas were she assertive, his vulnerability might become very apparent.

Useful reviews of physical illness and the family are provided by Lask [41,42]. What is clear, as mentioned by Weakland [43], is that the relationship between illness and disease and a family interactional view deserves more attention and research than it has so far received.

In the Family Therapy literature, there are many references to therapeutic approaches in work with families containing an ill member. To a greater or lesser degree, these practitioners treat the illness symptom as part of the family's pattern for coping rather than as an isolated, unrelated phenomenon. I will list some of the work in this field. Most practitioners and researchers would agree that more research is needed to provide conclusive evidence, although at the time of writing, findings on treating anorexic patients are shortly to be published from a research project at the Institute of Psychiatry and the Maudsley Hospital, London. The first paper [44] deals with the question of the relationship between systematic observation of family interaction sequences and clinical insight. Palazzoli [45] has charted her move from an individual intraphysic approach to a systems interactional approach in work with anorexic patients. Her work is further developed in Palazzoli et al. [23]. Minuchin and his colleagues [46] have described their approach to dealing with families containing anorexic patients. In the first part of their book they provide interesting data on the relationship between emotional arousal, by measuring the free-fatty-acid level in all members of families with a diabetic member, and lability in the diagnosed diabetic patient. It is unfortunate, however, that they do not give information which would allow replication of their study. The results as reported indicate a relationship between emotional arousal and psychosomatic crisis. 'Physiological evidence could be shown to support family psychological hypotheses...(there is strong support for) the hypothesis that the illness plays a role in these families. Parental arousal can be alleviated by the participation of the child, but only at the expense of symptom maintenance' [46].

The effect and treatment of other specific illnesses from a family perspective are provided in relation to: asthma (Lask and Kirk [47]); epilepsy (Ferrari, Matthews and Barabas [48]); deafness (Harvey [49]); chronic illness in adolescents (Frey [50]); schizophrenia (Lieberman and Goepfert [51]); and eczema (Loader, Kinston and Stratford [52]).

Thus, although it is important to focus on and understand the implications of illness for families, it is also important to be aware that things are not always what they seem in family life. Illness may represent a loss for the individual. It may also become the source of tyranny which dominates a whole family 'because so-and-so is ill' and loss of function for other family members can be insidiously all-pervasive. As Lask and Lask [53] comment, the reasons why a problem begins and why it persists are not necessarily the same. Illness can become a career for the individual which is more handicapping for others than the sufferer himself.

SOME OTHER FORMULATIONS OF LOSS

In this final section, I draw attention to other elements in family life which are normative parts of the family life cycle (see Carter and McGoldrick [54] for a good introductory text on the life cycle, and see Walsh [55] and Handel [56] for excellent collections of papers considering the family from a wide range of theoretical and scientific perspectives) and those which are paranormative. By paranormative, I mean those events which are not necessarily predictable. In this latter context, I have already considered studies on death and bereavement, both as part of the life cycle and as interruptions to the 'normal course of events'. The aim is to draw attention to the wide area of human experience which can be viewed from the perspective of loss. This theme is of course already familiar in the psychoanalytic literature, where the concept of loss is important in theories of the personality.

Normative Loss

At a very general level we might construe the whole of human development as revolving around the theme of loss, from the moment the infant leaves its mother's womb: mother and baby both lose something at this first separation. From then onwards, attempts are made to re-establish intimacy in the face of developmental losses through childhood, adolescence, young adulthood, and so on. The family life cycle literature focusses on these issues, and Haley [57] has described the work of Milton Erickson within this broad framework. There are those families familiar to social workers and other professionals where the woman never seems so fulfilled as when she is pregnant; and those families where a new child is born at about the time that the next eldest starts school. There are families where children seem to be born to 'replace' a child lost through death, and bearing the same name, or to replace a child removed by the authorities because of professional concerns about protection.

It is tempting to talk of normal family development, yet clearly there are many variations, due to culture, ethnic origin, economic conditions, or mishap. Various authors have attempted to understand these processes: for example, Goldberg [58], Bott [59], Kantor and Lehr [60], Lewis et al. [61] and Barcai [62]. Such attempts give us an idea of the extent of the problem. The 'typical' normative losses of someone in middle age can be represented schematically as in Figure 1.

FIGURE 1

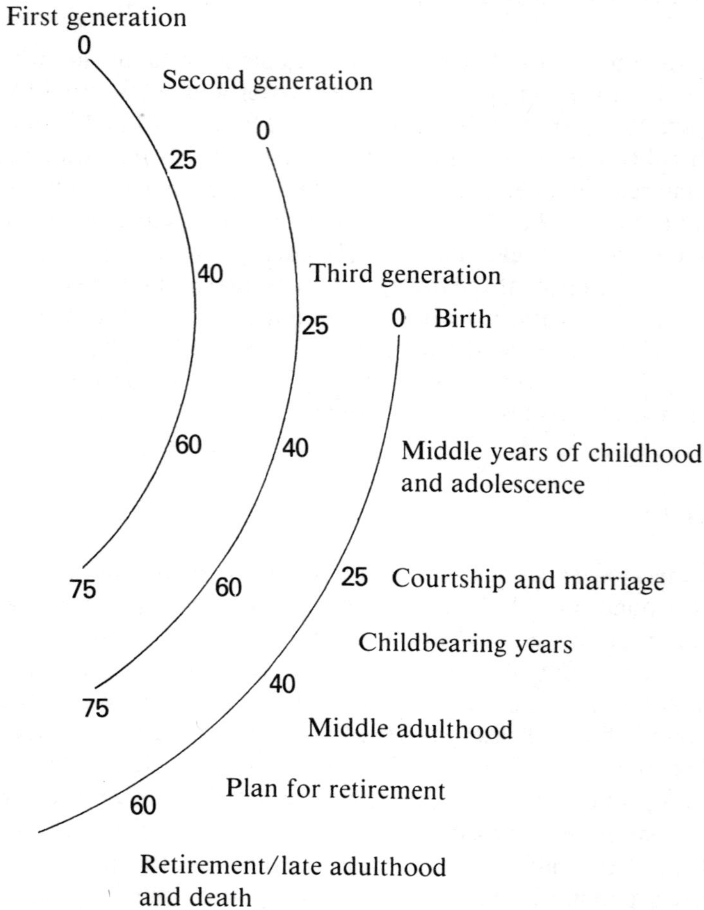

If each curve represents an individual's life span, the person on the second generation curve at age about 40 years plus can be construed as facing three kinds of loss. First, the loss of physical and mental powers of his parents, where they possibly need care in their own right, and can expect to be facing death. Second, the loss of his own children as they become young adults and begin to make their own more independent lives. And third, a realisation for the individual that he is probably at the peak of his physical and intellectual powers, and that he is unlikely to make great future advances in terms of a better job or promotion prospects. This explanation may give some understanding of the mid-life crisis from a three-generation developmental viewpoint.

The particular areas of normative loss which create difficulties for society are those of adolescence and old age. Useful references on adolescence are: Rutter et al. [63] to provide an overview, while writers who focus on practice issues within a developmental framework include: Berkowitz [64] ; Haley [3] ; Jenkins [4] ; and Kraemer [65]. In the area of old age, good references are: Berezin and Cath [66] ; Kubler-Ross [67] ; and Brody [68]. Approaches to working with the elderly and their families and dealing with loss are provided by Berezin and Cath [66]; Weisman [69]; and Herr and Weakland [70].

Paranormative Loss

Many events may happen to individuals and their families, that are not necessarily predictable, including severe illness which has already been covered. Some events, such as divorce and remarriage, are more common now than they were 50 years ago, although as Stone [71] points out, marriages and family continuity have always been liable to interruption. The difference is that now it is more likely to be through some degree of choice, rather than through early death. As Wiley [72] points out, we have witnessed considerable changes even in the past 30 years in our attitudes to the shape of the family. Some of the major problems encountered in step-families, also referred to in the literature as reconstituted or blended families, stem from difficulties associated with loss. All step-families are born of loss or 'failure'. Many step-parents attempt to become instant parents to their new children, even attempting to be better than the original parent. The adults also suffer a loss of something they never had together, namely the opportunity to be a couple without parenting responsibilities. Although the reasons for referral to helping agencies will be varied, it is likely in a high proportion where there has been a remarriage that some of the underlying difficulties relate to loss, and a failure to grieve for the family that was not, in an attempt to save the family that could be. The literature on problems that step-families encounter and methods of helping is increasing rapidly. Some references which deal with various aspects of these difficulties are: Robinson [73,74]; Visher and Visher [75]; Jenkins and Cowley [76] and Sager et al. [77]. An excellent review of the literature is provided by Bergquist [78].

The other discrete subject area to be mentioned is that of sexual abuse and incest. This again is an area of work which has received increasing interest in the past five years. It figures in interest much as the early work of Kempe in the 1960s when suddenly child physical abuse was 'discovered' as an identifiable syndrome. Jenkins and Cowley [76] comment in their brief paper on aspects of working with adolescents that: 'We may interpret 'loss of parental images' physically, psychologically, or both. It seems to us that extreme loss may be by death, physical rejection, or by a violation of generational boundaries through sexual interference.' The theme of loss and incest has been explored by Gutheil and Avery[79]. Mrazek and Kempe[80] have collected a series of papers which review the incidence of child sexual abuse and incest, and describe various intervention programmes. Renvoize[81] examines incest as a family pattern, and Pittman[82], Furniss[83] and Will[84] all describe issues related to treating the family where 'losses' of this nature have occurred. The loss is of generational boundaries, of basic trust between members of an intimate group, as much between child and adult as between adult sexual partners.

In conclusion, it is worth considering any presentation which involves a change, abrupt or otherwise, from the familiar, as comprising, at least in part, elements of loss. Folklore has it that a house move is one of the three most traumatic events in a family's life. It may mean the uprooting of all that is familiar for territory that is totally strange. The difficulties and disturbance, whether of acting out or failure to settle in the children, of a wife's non-specific symptoms of feeling depressed, or of a husband's sudden inability to cope, may all be responses to loss and an aspect of grieving the old while grappling with the new. These issues are particularly germane when working with immigrant families who have come to this country in the hope of a better life but experience considerable difficulties of acculturation[85]. Part of the difficulty of adopting the new relates to fear of letting go of the old, wherein identity and a sense of being rooted are under threat. The real implications of such loss may only begin to be experienced as children in the family adopt the host culture's mores in opposition to parental values.

DISCUSSION

In this chapter I have linked a few formal studies which consider various aspects of loss through death of the individual and the family. I then reviewed some of the issues related to treatment. The next most obvious category was that of illness, and effects on those most involved. What I have indicated in the last main section is that 'loss' as a generic concept is useful and applicable in many situations which face professional helpers. However, the issues of loss are often less immediately obvious. What are the issues around loss as a new family attempts to form from the disappointment of failed hopes that a previous marriage represents? What is the loss of trust that a child experiences when subject to sexual (or physical) abuse? The implications may be far-reaching as that person in later life chooses a mate and attempts to parent in his or her own right. Children who have been raised in institutions suffer a loss of skills as parents – a loss in the sense that they may never have had the opportunity to experience them as recipients in their own development86. Families that struggle with a handicapped member may never have the opportunity to mourn the loss of the healthy child that never was [87].

At a more mundane level, the struggles which families with adolescent members go through also relate to issues of loss – loss of the 'child' becoming an adult, loss perhaps of the status of parent and the crisis of renegotiating primarily a spouse role [88]. In a similar way, it may be that many of the so-called chaotic, under-organised families, as described by Minuchin et al. [89], are families which have 'lost' an effective generation which professional agencies are called upon to fill [90].

There is a sense in which the topic of loss and the family is inexhaustible. It would be unwise to stretch the concept too far. And yet it may be that we have failed to understand precisely how pervasive an issue it is. It is relatively simple to transpose models for formal grief-work from bereavement studies to the reactions of children placed in foster care or children's homes, or on admission to hospital. It is perhaps not always so easy to see how loss, which may be of something that never has been experienced in the first instance, is an important underlying theme in the experience of people who come for help with a variety of otherwise apparently unrelated problems. Many of the references have been heavily slanted towards the individual, or the condition, in the context where it occurs, which most often is the family. Although no two families are identical there is sufficient overlap, given cultural and socio-economic factors, to be able to generalise with some degree of certainty. One of the important factors is the stage of the family life cycle when events take place or around which they cluster. Any interruption to what the members perceive for them as 'the normal life cycle', will represent 'loss' in some form or other.

References

1. Finkelhor, D. 'Common Features of Family Abuse'. In Finkelhor, D., Gelles, R.J., Hotaling, G.T. & Straus, M.A. (Eds.) *The Dark Side of Families*. Sage Publications, London, 1983, 17-28.

2. Haley, J. *Problem-Solving Therapy*. Harper and Row, London, 1976.

3. Haley, J. *Leaving Home: the Therapy of Disturbed Young People*. McGraw Hill, New York, 1980.

4. Jenkins, H. 'Can I (let you let me) Leave? Therapy with the Adolescent and His Family' *Journal of Family Therapy*. 3, 1981, 113-138.

5. Parkes, C.M. 'Bereavement and Mental Illness. Part 1. A Clinical Study of the Grief of Bereaved Psychiatric Patients' *British Journal of Medical Psychology*. 38, 1965, 1-12.

6. Lieberman, S. 'Nineteen Cases of Morbid Grief' *British Journal of Psychiatry*. 132, 1978, 159-163.

7. Parkes, C.M. 'Bereavement and Mental Illness. Part 2. A Classification of Bereavement Reactions' *British Journal of Medical Psychology*. 38, 1965, 13-26.

8. Fried, M. 'Grieving for a Lost Home'. In Dahl, L.J. (Ed.) *The Environment of the Metropolis*. Basic Books, New York, 1962.

9. Fisher, S.H. 'Psychiatric Considerations of Hand Disability' *Archives of Physical Medicine and Rehabilitation*. 41, 1960, 62.

10. Lindemann, E. 'Symptomatology and Management of Acute Grief' *American Journal of Psychiatry*. 101, 1944, 141-148.

11. Bowlby, J. 'Childhood Mourning and its Implications for Psychiatry' *American Journal of Psychiatry*. 118, 1961, 481-498.

12. Garmezy, N. & Rutter, M. 'Acute Reactions to Stress'. In Rutter, M. & Hersov, L. (Eds.) *Child and Adolescent Psychiatry: Modern Approaches*. Second Edition, Blackwell Scientific, Oxford, 1985, 152-176.

13. Gleser, G.L., Green, B.L. & Winget, C. *Prolonged Psycho-social Effects of Disaster: A Study of Buffalo Creek*. Academic Press, New York, 1981.

14. Birtchnell, J. Personal Communication. 1985.

15. Birtchnell, J. 'Early Parent Death and Mental Illness' *British Journal of Psychiatry*. 116, 1970, 281-288.

16. Birtchnell, J. 'Depression in Relation to Early and Recent Parent Death' *British Journal of Psychiatry*. 116, 197O, 299-306.

17. Malan, D.H. *Individual Psychotherapy and the Science of Psycho-dynamics*. Butterworths, London, 1979.

18. Brown, G.W., Harris, T. & Copeland, J.R. 'Depression and Loss' *British Journal of Psychiatry*. 130, 1977, 1-18.

19. Pincus, L. *Death and the Family*. Faber, London, 1976.

20. Parkes, C.M. 'Bereavement Counselling: Does it Work?' *British Medical Journal*. 281, 5 July 1980, 3-6.

21. Lieberman, S. *Transgenerational Family Therapy*. Croom Helm, London, 1979.

22. Lieberman, S. 'A Transgenerational Theory' *Journal of Family Therapy*. 1, 1979, 347-360.

23. Palazzoli, M.S., Cecchin, G., Prata, G. & Boscolo, L. *Paradox and Counter-paradox*. Jason Aronson, New York, 1978.

24. Paul, N.L. 'The Role of Mourning and Empathy in Conjoint Marital Therapy'. In Zuk, G.H. & Boszormenyi-Nagy, I. (Eds.) *Family Therapy and Disturbed Families*. Science Books, New York, 1967, 186-205.

25. Minuchin, S. *Families and Family Therapy*. London, Tavistock, 1974.

26. Palazzoli, M.S., Boscolo, L., Cecchin, G.F. & Prata, G. 'Family Rituals: A Powerful Tool in Family Therapy' *Family Process*. 16, 1977, 445-453.

27. Ferreira, A.J. 'Family Myth and Homeostasis' *Archives of General Psychiatry*. 9, 1963, 457-473.

28. Byng-Hall, J. 'Family Myths as a Defence in Conjoint Family Therapy' *British Journal of Medical Psychology*. 46, 1973, 239-250.

29. Pattison, E.M. 'The Fatal Myth of Death in the Family' *American Journal of Psychiatry*. 133, 1976, 674-678.

30. Paul, N.L. & Paul, B.B. 'Death and Changes in Sexual Behaviour'. In Walsh, F. (Ed.) *Normal Family Processes*. Guiford Press, New York, 1982, 229-250.

31. Black, D. 'Mourning and the Family'. In Walrond-Skinner, S. (Ed.) *Developments in Family Therapy*. Routledge and Kegan Paul, London, 1981, 189-201.

32. Bowlby-West, L. 'The Impact of Death on the Family System' *Journal of Family Therapy*. 5, 1983, 279-294.

33. Gelcer, E. 'Mourning is a Family Affair' *Family Process*. 22, 1983, 501-516.

34. Herz, F. 'The Impact of Death and Serious Illness on the Family'. In Carter, E.A. & McGoldrick, M. (Eds.) *The Family Life Cycle: A Framework for Family Therapy*. Gardner Press, New York, 1980, 223-240.

35. Heard, D. 'From Object Relations to Attachment Theory: A Basis for Family Therapy' *British Journal of Medical Psychology*. 51, 1978, 67-76.

36. Lieberman, S. & Black, D. 'Loss, Mourning and Grief'. In Bentovim, A., Gorell-Barnes, G. & Cooklin, A. (Eds.) *Family Therapy: Complementary Frameworks in Theory and Practice*. Vol. 2, Academic Press, London, 1982, 373-387.

37. Lewis, E. & Page, A. 'Failure to Mourn a Stillbirth: An Overlooked Catastrophe' *British Journal of Medical Psychology*. 51, 1978, 237-241.

38. Lewis, E. 'The Management of Stillbirth: Coping with an Unreality' *The Lancet*. 2, 1976, 619-620.

39. Meyer, R. & Lewis, E. 'The Impact of a Stillbirth on a Marriage' *Journal of Family Therapy*. 1, 1979, 361-369.

40. Grolnick, L. 'A Family Perspective of Psychosomatic Factors in Illness: A Review of the Literature' *Family Process*. 11, 1972, 457-486.

41. Lask, B. 'Illness in the Family'. In Walrond-Skinner, S. (Ed.) *Developments in Family Therapy*. Routledge and Kegan Paul, London, 1981, 167-188.

42. Lask, B. 'Physical Illness and the Family'. In Bentovim, A., Gorell-Barnes, G. & Cooklin, A. (Eds.) *Family Therapy: Complementary Frameworks in Theory and Practice*. 2, Academic Press, London, 1982, 441-461.

43. Weakland, J.H. 'Family Somatics: a Neglected Edge' *Family Process*. 16, 1977, 263-272.

44. Eisler, I., Szmukler, G.I. & Dare, C. 'Systematic Observation and Clinical Insight – Are They Compatible? An Experiment in Recognising Family Interactions' *Psychological Medicine*. 15, 1985, 173-188.

45. Palazzoli, M.S. *Self-Starvation*. Human Context Books, London, 1974.

46. Minuchin, S., Rosman, B. & Baker, L. *Psychosomatic Families: Anorexia Nervosa in Context*. Harvard University Press, Cambridge, Mass., 1978.

47. Lask, B. & Kirk, M. 'Childhood Asthma: Family Therapy as an Adjunct to Routine Management' *Journal of Family Therapy*. 1, 1979, 33-48.

48. Ferrari, M., Matthews, W.S. & Barabas, G. 'The Family and Child with Epilepsy' *Family Process*. 22, 1983, 53-59.

49. Harvey, M.A. 'Family Therapy with Deaf Persons: the Systematic Utilisation of an Interpreter'. *Family Process*. 23, 1984, 205-221.

50. Frey, J. 'A Family/Systems Approach to Illness-Maintaining Behaviours in Chronically Ill Adolescents' *Family Process*. 23, 1984, 251-260.

51. Lieberman, S. & Goepfert, M. 'Clarity: the Management of Families of the Schizophrenic Syndrome' *Journal of Family Therapy*. 5, 1983, 307-320.

52. Loader, P., Kinston, W. & Stratford, J. 'Is There a 'Psychosomatogenic' Family?' *Journal of Family Therapy*. 2, 1980, 311-326.

53. Lask, J. & Lask, B. *Child Psychiatry & Social Work*. Tavistock, London, 1981.

54. Carter, E.A. & McGoldrick, M. (Eds.) *The Family Life Cycle: A Framework for Family Therapy*. Gardner Press, New York, 1980.

55. Walsh, F. (Ed.) *Normal Family Processes*. Guilford Press, New York, 1982.

56. Handel, G. (Ed.) *The Psychosocial Interior of the Family*. Aldine, New York, 1985.

57. Haley, J. *Uncommon Therapy*. Norton, New York, 1973.

58. Goldberg, E.M. 'The Normal Family – Myth and Reality'. In Younghusband, E. (Ed.) *Social Work with Families*. George Allen and Unwin, London, 1965, 11-27.

59. Bott, E. *Family and Social Network*. Tavistock, Social Science Paperback, London, 1957.

60. Kantor, D. & Lehr, W. *Inside the Family: Toward a Theory of Family Process*. Jossey-Bass, San Francisco, 1975.

61. Lewis, J.M., Bevers, W.R., Gossett, J.T. & Phillips, V.A. *No Single Thread: Psychological Health in Family Systems*. Brunner/Mazel, New York, 1976.

62. Barcai, A. 'Normative Family Development' *Journal of Marital and Family Therapy*. 7, 1981, 353-359.

63. Rutter, M., Graham, P., Chadwick, O.F.D. & Yule, W. 'Adolescent Turmoil: Fact or Fiction?' *Journal of Child Psychology and Psychiatry*. 17, 1976, 35-56.

64. Berkowitz, D.A. 'The Disturbed Adolescent and his Family: Problems of Individuation' *Journal of Adolescence*. 2, 1979, 27-39.

65. Kraemer, S. 'Leaving Home and the Adolescent Family Therapist' *Journal of Adolescence*. 5, 1982, 51-62.

66. Berezin, M.A. & Cath, S.H. (Eds.) *Geriatric Psychiatry: Grief, Loss and Emotional Disorder in the Aging Process*. International Universities Press, New York, 1965.

67. Kubler-Ross, E. *On Death and Dying*. MacMillan, London, 1969.

68. Brody, E.H. 'Aging and Family Personality: A Developmental View' *Family Process*. 13, 1974, 23-28.

69. Weisman, A.D. 'The Psychiatric and the Geriatric Patient. Partial Grief in Family Members and others who Care for the Elderly Patient. Discussion' *Journal of Geriatric Psychiatry*. 3, 197O, 65-69.

70. Herr, J.J. & Weakland, J.H. *Counselling Elders and their Families*. Springer Publishing Co., New York, 1979.

71. Stone,L. *The Family, Sex and Marriage in England 1500-1800*. Penguin Books, Harmondsworth, 1979.

72. Wiley, N. 'Marriage and the Construction of Reality: Then and Now'. In Handel, G. (Ed.) *The Psychosocial Interior of the Family*. Aldine, London, 1985, 21-32.

73. Robinson, M. 'Step-families: A Reconstituted Family System' *Journal of Family Therapy*. 2, 1980, 45-69.

74. Robinson, M. 'Reconstituted Families: Some Implications for the Family Therapy'. In Bentovim, A., Gorell-Barnes, G. & Cooklin, A. (Eds.) *Family Therapy: Complementary Frameworks for Theory and Practice*. Vol. 2, Academic Press, London, 1982, 389-415.

75. Visher, E.B. & Visher, J.S. 'Step-families are Different' *Journal of Family Therapy*. 7, 1985, 9-18.

76. Jenkins, H. and Cowley, J. 'Adolescents in Crisis: On Hypothesising with Minimal Information' *British Journal of Social Work*. 15, 1985, 351-362.

77. Sager, C.J., Brown, H.S., Crohn, H., Engel, T., Rodstein, E. & Walker, L. *Treating the Remarried Family*. Brunner/Mazel, New York, 1983.

78. Bergquist, B. 'The Remarried Family: An Annotated Bibliography' *Family Process*. 23, 1984, 107-119.

79. Gutheil, T.G. & Avery, N.C. 'Multiple Overt Incest as Family Defence against Loss' *Family Process*. 16, 1977, 105-116.

80. Mrazek, P.B. & Kempe, C.H. (Eds.) *Sexually Abused Children and their Families*. Pergamon Press, New York, 1981.

81. Renvoize, J. *Incest: A Family Pattern*. Routledge & Kegan Paul, London, 1982.

82. Pittman, F.S. III. 'Incest'. In Masserman, J.H. (Ed.) *Current Psychiatric Therapies*. Vol. 17, Grune & Stratton, New York, 1977, 129-134.

83. Furniss, T. 'Family Process in the Treatment of IntraFamilial Child Sexual Abuse' *Journal of Family Therapy*. 5, 1983, 263-278.

84. Will, D. 'Approaching the Incestuous and Sexually Abusive Family' *Journal of Adolescence*. 6, 1983, 229-246.

85. Sluzki, C.E. 'Migration and Family Conflict' *Family Process*. 18, 1979, 379-390.

86. Dowdney, L., Skuse, D., Rutter, M., Quinton, D. & Mrazek, D. 'The Nature and Qualities of Parenting Provided by Women Raised in Institutions' *Journal of Child Psychology and Psychiatry*. 26, 1985, 599-625.

87. Black, D. 'Handicap and Family Therapy'. In Bentovim, A., Gorell-Barnes, G. & Cooklin, A. (Eds.) *Family Therapy: Complementary Frameworks of Theory and Practice*. Vol. 2, Academic Press, London, 1982, 417-439.

88. Dare, C. 'The Empty Nest: Families with Older Adolescents and Models of Family Therapy'. In Bentovim, A., Gorell-Barnes, G. & Cooklin, A. (Eds.) *Family Therapy: Complementary Frameworks of Theory and Practice*. Vol. 2, Academic Press, London, 1982, 3[illegible]3-359.

89. Minuchin, S., Montalvo, B., Guerney, B.C., Rosman, B.L. & Schumer, F. *Families of the Slums*. Basic Books, New York, 1967.

90. Jenkins, H. 'A Life Cycle Framework in the Treatment of Under-Organised Families' *Journal of Family Therapy*. 5, 1983, 359-377.

Disturbed Relationships

Douglas Chisholm

INTRODUCTION

This chapter looks at how families with disturbed relationships present themselves to helping agencies, and at the variety of ways that individual symptomatology and disturbed family relationships may be linked. How the same problems may be treated in a variety of different ways is discussed and some of the considerations that should be attended to in arriving at a treatment package are indicated. The chapter is written from the point of view of a child and adolescent psychiatrist and there is, therefore, an emphasis on relationship problems in families who might be seen at a Department of Child and Family Psychiatry. However, this does not mean that adult disturbance is not considered; children of families with a disturbed parent are themselves more at risk of being disturbed [1], and work with these families is an essential part of the practice of child and adolescent psychiatry.

THE COMPLAINT

1. In Relationship Terms or 'We Have a Problem'

A proportion of families who require help because of disturbed relationships will come for help describing their problem themselves in relationship terms. The most frequent such presentation among adults is, of course, as a marital problem (though, by no means, would all couples who wish help with their marriages accept that both of them are playing a part in their difficulties). Very much overlapping with this are sexual problems. When a marriage has broken down irretrievably, too, the couple may recognise that they still require help, so as to achieve:

(a) as amicable a divorce as possible, and

(b) as satisfactory a relationship as possible afterwards, since contact after formal proceedings are over often continues to be necessary. The Finer Report (1974)[2] first brought conciliation into prominence as a way of meeting these needs.

Parents and children, too, may come for help feeling that something has gone wrong between them. Usually, even when both conceptualise the problem in this way, and, of course, young children are not able to do so, the parent will be the one who has taken the initiative. Occasionally, however, an adolescent will have been the prime mover. Parents, too, will at times seek help because they perceive their children's relationships with each other as unsatisfactory – most often too aggressive and quarrelsome.

2. As Another's Responsibility or 'It's Him (or Her)'

As has already been hinted with reference to marital problems, even when a person recognises that what is happening between himself* and another is problematic, that does not mean he accepts that he has much responsibility for what is happening. Often he may feel his symptoms are the result of the other's illness, disability or unreasonable behaviour. For example, an adolescent may see his rebelliousness as a necessary response to his parents' rigidities without seeing that some of his behaviour is provoking parents to become even more rigid; or a mother may feel her depression to be the inevitable consequence of the pressure of coping with a hyperactive toddler, without seeing that her depressed lack of involvement with the child is exacerbating his hyperactivity as he tries desperately to gain her attention. Framo[3], too, has commented with regard to marital therapy that most people enter this to change their mate.

3. As Individual Symptomatogy or 'I am Ill' or 'I Have Got a Problem' or 'My Child Has..... '

The majority of approaches for help are couched in terms of individual symptomatology. Any of the symptoms of psychiatric disorder may be presented in this way – depression, anxiety, phobia and alcohol abuse – would

*The male pronoun is used for the sake of brevity.

be just a few of the more common presenting complaints with adults. Temper tantrums, sleep difficulties, stealing, misbehaviour in school, slow progress at reading and school refusal are a few of the forms of disturbed behaviour that lead to children being brought for help. Even with these few examples it is clear that it is not only to doctors, including psychiatrists, that individuals with these problems come, but to social workers, educational psychologists, guidance teachers and others; and it is clear that not all such individuals are suffering from psychiatric disorder but that all these 'symptoms' may well be associated with disturbed relationships.

4. As a Problem Unrelated to Disturbed Relationships or 'It is Something Else'

All three types of presentations described so far are widely (though by no means universally) recognised as indicating a need for some attention to be paid to family relationships. There are other presentations, however, that carry a greater risk of underlying relationship difficulties not even being considered. Firstly, there are individuals who respond to their difficulties by developing problems that appear to require 'practical' remedies: prison for fraud in response to a wife's nagging over money; operation for peptic ulceration from tension in the family; financial help and advice on budgeting when the family have their electricity cut off because of parents' inability to co-operate even to the extent of agreeing how the bills are paid. The risk of attention not being paid to the disturbed relationships in these families is increased by it being not unlikely that they will be dealt with by someone whose main concerns are far removed from treating disturbed relationships, e.g. a surgeon or a social security officer.

Secondly, there are families where the help is being sought but without the family being in agreement or fully aware of what they want help with, or the family may have some awareness that they require help with their relationships but they may be more than usually ambivalent about seeking such help. There are a number of reasons for this, such as fear of criticism fuelled by feelings of guilt and fear of the unknown, including the feeling 'better the devil you know'; changed relationships are not necessarily more satisfying ones. This can lead to the requests for help being somewhat obscure. For example, a mother's saying to her family doctor that her six-year-old son won't eat green vegetables, could reflect an isolated food fad but could be her way of requesting help because her son was disobedient with her and her husband unsupportive [4]. Balint [5] describes how patients put their complaints into terms that they believe will be acceptable to their doctor, and how there is then what amounts to a process of negotiation between the patient and the doctor until a problem or illness is agreed on. Kanner [6] talks of symptoms in terms of an admission ticket for help.

It is likely that a similar process occurs between other caregivers and their clients: requests to social workers for help with financial problems and for rehousing may be of this nature. It is likely that requests for help with emotional problems, which will very frequently include relationship problems, are commonly missed. That some of these missed requests are serious is suggested by statistics showing the high proportion of individuals who have consulted their family doctor before self-poisoning or self-injury [7], and the number of children who have been brought to hospital with apparently little wrong before they are physically abused [8].

THE RELATIONSHIP OF INDIVIDUAL SYMPTOMATOLOGY TO DISTURBED FAMILY RELATIONSHIPS

Since the largest proportion of approaches for help will be with the problems seen in individual terms, it is now proposed to examine the relationship of individual symptomatology to disturbed family relationships in more detail.

(a) In some families the problems of the person referred, i.e. the identified patient, are an expression of the family's dysfunction. To understand how this occurs, it is useful to keep in mind that a family operates as a set of mutually inter-dependent units, i.e. a system which has powerful influences on the behaviour and experience of each individual; and, in return, the individual member influences the behaviour and experiences of the other members of the system. The individual comes to attention when the family is having difficulty in coping, either with inside stress coming from developmental changes in its own members, or outside stress from the demands of other systems with which the family is involved, or from the impact of life events such as illness or bereavement. John and his family (see below) might well be viewed as falling into this group.

(b) In another group of families the primary part of the problem lies with the identified patient, but it is still important to consider the impact of the problem on the family and how the family will influence the outcome for the identified patient, for better or for worse. For example, families with a mentally handicapped child may require a great deal of support in coping with the pressures and problems that arise and in coming to terms with their child's handicap, and a family-based approach to psychotherapy may be the most appropriate [9]. Broadly similar statements can be made about families with a member suffering from a wide range of illnesses and disabilities – autism, hyperkinetic syndrome, schizoid personality, brain damage (including road accident victims), senile and pre-senile dementia, mania and some cases of depression, and, of course, when there is a physically ill or handicapped member. For families with a schizophrenic member, too, the view that, although the schizophrenic illness should not be regarded as primarily or mainly a result or expression of pathological family interactions, the onset, course and prognosis are likely to be *influenced* by the nature of the family interactions, is proving increasingly productive[10,11].

(c) With disturbed children and adolescents, it is often easy to see how the child's problems stemmed in the first place from disturbed family relationships, but by the time the child is seen, he has, to a major extent, problems in his own right. At one time there was a tendency to consider this to be generally the case, as the disturbed child's problems were viewed as reflecting disordered personality development that was relatively independent of the environment. Now it is widely recognised that a child's behaviour is much more responsive to the environment than that view would have indicated, but it still remains the case in many children (and adolescents) and, by the time they come to attention, will show evidence of persistent disturbance in a variety of environments with which they could reasonably be expected to cope.

In other families the identified patient is sent (or brought, if a child) as a messenger to get help for the family as a whole or for some part of the family. The authority of the parents relative to the child or adolescent means that a child or adolescent is often the family member chosen for this role.

These groupings reflect different parts of a continuum rather than discrete entities and they are not, by any means, mutually exclusive. Indeed, it would be the rule rather than the exception for the individual symptomatology to be related to the disturbed family relationships in more than one way, even though one might predominate.

ALTERNATIVE APPROACHES TO TREATMENT

John, aged six years, was referred because of headaches. When he had these headaches he made a great fuss and his mother was quick to go to him to comfort him. At other times, he was a quiet, well-behaved child who did not go out a lot. He did not seem to have friends in his neighbourhood. Only John and his mother attended the initial appointment, although father had also been invited to attend. He was said to be too busy to get off work. The relationship between John and his mother seemed to be a close one and, while she was there, he seemed reasonably relaxed. However, he was reluctant to talk to the male psychiatrist and became very anxious when the psychiatrist wished to see him on his own. Although his mother was able to persuade him to stay, he remained tense throughout the individual session. Some hints of the nature of the underlying difficulties emerged from a family drawing in which he drew himself between his father, much the largest figure, and his mother and from a statement that he did nothing with his father. Further enquiries of mother revealed that father demanded that her attention should be focused on him when he was at home and that he treated John strictly and with little patience. It was clear from what mother said that she felt that John's 'illness' was the only justification for her spending time with John, that father felt unable to resist.

How could this case be treated? An individual psychotherapeutic approach would involve John being seen for play therapy with collateral counselling or psychotherapy with parents. In play therapy, John would benefit from experiences of total acceptance, empathic understanding and from being helped to express and understand, through his play, his angry feelings towards his father and his desire for closeness with his mother. As therapy progressed, too, he might also become aware of feelings of resentment of his mother for her fussing and more positive feelings towards his father. In counselling, mother might be able to change her submissiveness to her husband and her rushing to comfort John, by using her relationship with her worker as a secure base where pent-up feelings could be expressed and where she could explore changes in her attitudes[12]. She might, however, also benefit from psychodynamic psychotherapy, as it seems likely that her attitudes reflected the intrusion into current relationships of unresolved conflicts linked with disturbed childhood relationships. For example, her relationship with her husband was similar to the relationship she had had with her father, and to re-experience and learn to understand that earlier relationship in a transference to a therapist might allow her to behave differently to her husband – and so to her son. If father could be involved in counselling or psychotherapy, possibly together with his wife, it might help him to modify his behaviour. Marital therapy seems an alternative since, if John's mother felt she had a more equal relationship with her husband, the quality of the marriage might improve, and father would feel more secure and more able to allow his wife to spend time with John instead of with him.

Behaviour therapy would be an alternative approach to treatment. For example, behaviour therapy might involve John being rewarded by mother's attention for not complaining of headaches and ignored by mother when he did complain.

Conjoint family therapy seemed another possibility. It would allow opportunities for interventions aimed at directly modifying the functioning of the whole family. For example, the therapist might choose to focus on problems in communication in the family since, if the family members could communicate better, further improvements would follow. The therapist might note that when John wanted something, if he asked his father he was usually ignored and he would then interrupt parents' conversation to make his request of his mother in a whining voice, to father's great annoyance. The therapist might intervene to draw to father's attention that he was missing John's approach and get John and father to negotiate so that John would approach father in a way that was acceptable to father and that father would then respond. Mother could be asked to join father in making it clear to John about making his request to father rather than to her. The therapist might also note that John sat between parents, closer to mother. He might move John from that position, perhaps to sit beside him in the first place, and direct parents to discuss some issue, moving them closer together perhaps facing each other. If John tried to interrupt he would stop him doing so. These interventions might be viewed as first steps towards helping John and father to develop a more involved and positive relationship, towards helping mother to support that change and to change her own relationship with John and towards clarifying for the family that it was not appropriate for John to come between his parents, either physically or verbally.

To take further the consideration of how it comes about that apparently widely different forms of intervention can all prove beneficial, it is helpful to return to looking at the family as a system. This implies that changes in one subsystem – the children, the parents, the marital couple or individuals – tend to induce changes in other parts of the system. For example, in John's family, if father changes by becoming less demanding of mother, then it is likely to affect not only his relationship with his wife, but also the other family relationships as well. As regards John's presenting symptoms, John may then abandon these as with mother being freer to attend to him, he has less need to gain her attention through complaints of headaches. This does not imply, however, that father's demandingness should be seen as the cause of John's symptoms. In evaluating how a family can best be helped, it is usually useful to consider causality as a circular process. This is illustrated for John's family by the following diagram, from which it will be clear that it is possible to take any point in the circle and see what is occurring there as stemming from the other interactions in the circle and as, in turn, giving rise to these.

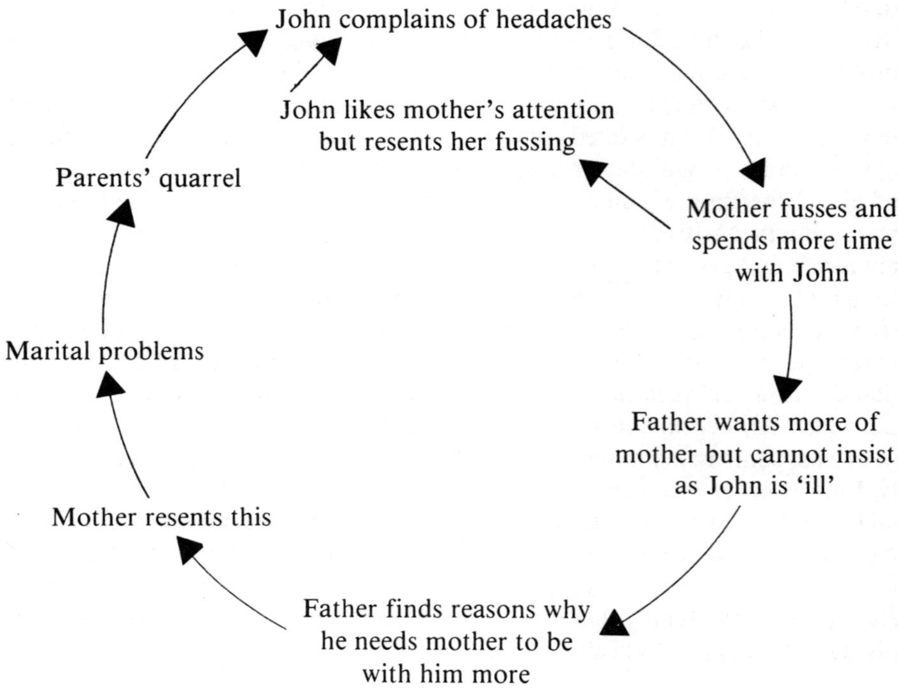

It follows from what has been said that an intervention at any point in the system may bring about changes in another part of the system. It is likely that in many cases improvement and, certainly, lasting improvement is conditional on these changes taking place. In John's case, therefore, to consider the behaviour therapy option, if this were to be successful it would entail not only changing mother's and John's behaviour but also father becoming able to tolerate mother being more involved with John for reasons other than complaints of illness. That, in turn, might only be possible if the marital relationship improved (which it might well, of course, if father became less demanding of mother).

This raises the question of whether intervention at more than one point in a family system is necessary. There is good reason to think that it is not always necessary. With play therapy, Axline [13] has argued strongly, for example, that children whose parents are not willing or able to be involved can benefit from individual play therapy and, in her famous case, DIBS [14], indeed, the description of DIBS's interaction with his mother after a play therapy session is a vivid illustration of how such changes can occur. Slavson & Schiffer [15], talking about activity groups, have described 'transference in reverse' by which children, benefiting from activity group therapy, induce changes in their families as well. The successes reported by behaviour therapists, too, carry the same message. Having said that, it is clear that in many cases, intervention in more than one area is necessary. In the behaviour therapy management of John's case, for example, it was clear that involving father as well could well improve the chances of helpful changes in his relationship with his wife and John and that if marital problems were severe, marital therapy might well also be necessary. Douglas [16] has shown how techniques of behaviour modification can be influenced and extended by the use of a systems framework. With play therapy for John, too, a successful outcome would be more likely if this were combined with work with one or preferably both parents. Another reason for taking the whole family system into account, even if the presenting problem can be resolved by treatment of an individual subsystem, is that the effect of such a change on other parts of the system may not be beneficial, as Frude [17] has pointed out.

'Context or Client' or 'Context and Client'

Although considering the family as a system makes sense of the way in which a variety of treatment options can result in equal benefit, many family therapists would make the further conceptual leap of considering the whole family as their patient or client. The goal of family therapy then becomes a higher degree of functioning in the family system [18]. In some circumstances some families may come to a family therapist knowing that family therapy with that goal is what is on offer. More often the justification for offering a family therapy is that it is the most effective way to help the family with their problem, whether that is defined by the family in relationship terms or in other terms, such as individual symptomatology; and/or that, by achieving a higher degree of functioning, the family will both be better able to cope with the effects of some problem, e.g. the illness of one of the members, and be better able to meet the needs of its members, including the sick individual. With the goal of achieving a higher degree of functioning of the family system, many family therapists then examine in what ways the family system is dysfunctional and focus on ways of changing these dysfunctions, whether or not they directly involve the identified patient. Different family therapists would choose to focus on different aspects, depending on their model of healthy family functioning. For example, Satir [19] would focus on communication in the family and consider that when all the members of the family are able to communicate in a healthy way, the family is no longer dysfunctional. How a therapist might focus on communication has already been illustrated with John and his family. It is to be noted that the intervention described could be seen as restructuring, i.e. changing the 'patterns of how, when and to whom to relate' [20].

Despite considering the family as patient or client having proved productive in working with many families, it is always equally valid to view the family as the context of the individual member, and it would seem to be advantageous for a therapist to keep both perspectives in mind in working with families. Interventions may be chosen, too, on the basis of either perspective and, at times, the different perspectives may lead to different views, and a decision will then have to be made as to which should take precedence for that individual and that family.

Choice of Treatment

In this section, how a decision can be arrived at as regards the choice of treatment will be discussed, attending particularly to the issue of whether individual and/or family therapy is required. In the previous section, it was pointed out how successful treatment approaches concentrating on the individual or some other subsystem also changed the system, but it was not intended to imply that this was generally the case or that the choice between different approaches did not merit careful consideration. In general, indeed, as Haldane, Alexander & Walker [21] have pointed out, the worker has a responsibility to be aware of options for treatment and to consider the consequences of what is decided, including the risks, since treatment may not only be disturbing and distressing but can be harmful. In considering the options, the worker has to be clear about what he, himself, can offer and about what colleagues or other agencies have available. The writer would argue, too, that whether one views the family as the context or as the client, the worker has a responsibility to consider the effects of the intervention chosen on *all* the family members.

Clearly, a decision about choice of treatment depends on some form of assessment being made. As the range of problems linked with disturbed relationships is very wide, as are the ways in which families make contact with helping agencies, there can be no single approach to assessment that will be appropriate in all cases. In the first place, the worker has to aim to pick up as fully as possible the meaning of the initial contact by the individual or family. It is to be noted, too, that assessment is also the beginning of treatment and that the nature of the relationships established is more important than information-getting. Minuchin[20] emphasises this by his description of techniques for joining with the family and in his statement that these are successful when they ensure that the family returns for a second session. In the writer's work setting, the problem is most commonly presented in terms of the disturbed behaviour or emotional state of a child or adolescent. In such cases, information is usually available from a variety of sources and can be obtained with parents' permission, but the core of the assessment lies in the sessions with the child, the parents and the family. Physical or psychological investigations may also be sometimes necessary. The assessment should lead to a diagnosis in the sense of both a diagnostic classification and a diagnostic formulation.

Classification will apply to the child as there is, at present, no satisfactory diagnostic classification for parent-child interactions or disturbed families[22], although some attempts have been made[23]. Of course, if another family member is suffering from a psychiatric disorder, it is important that this is recognised. The diagnostic classification narrows the field as regards choice of treatment[24], but there is no close correspondence overall between diagnostic classification and treatment which has to be decided on in the light of the diagnostic formulation. The diagnostic formulation, attending to both psychological and biological factors, indicates how the problem came about and how it has been maintained in *this* child and *this* family, and should include strengths as well as problems. Most formulations concentrate on the individual child with the family considered as context to a variable extent. The emphasis placed on social/cultural aspects would also vary. In contrast, many family therapists concentrate on an assessment of the whole family, some paying little or no attention to individual psychopathology. The historical information about the family is considered important by some therapists, some of whom emphasise, however, that the history is 'for the family rather than for the therapist'[18]. Others would also be concerned with its more indirect value and the light it throws on family's problems which will inform the therapists' subsequent moves to help the family[19,25,26,27]. In assessment of the family, most family therapists place the heaviest emphasis on the current functioning of the family system, information being most often gathered mainly from the interaction of the family in the here and now of a whole family interview. Some family therapists choose not to concern themselves at all with assessment of the referred patient, on the basis that they would not use the information in therapy, that such an assessment tends to militate against a shift from the problem being seen as an individual one to it being seen as a family problem, and because of the risk of collusion. Assessment of other family members as individuals would not be undertaken either for similar reasons. However, it seems to the writer that this is acceptable practice, if applied across the board, only if the family and the referrer are aware that this is what the worker and agency offer, and individual assessments can be obtained elsewhere. In some cases, however, another worker's assessment of sufficient other information will be available so that an individual interview may be decided not to be necessary. In other cases, it may be decided after the conjoint interview that an individual interview is unnecessary. It is to be noted that, in effect, a limited form of individual assessment is then being done. It is important, too, that the worker clarifies the reasons for not carrying out a fuller assessment, since there is a risk that his decision not to do so stems from the psychopathology of the individual or family or from anxieties that have been evoked in the worker about undertaking that particular interview.

In most circumstances, therefore, a comprehensive assessment should encompass individual assessment of the referred patient, a family history and background, including an assessment of the family as a system, and an assessment of the socio-cultural context. These areas should be covered and integrated in the diagnostic formulation. Such dimensions as Minuchin's [20] 'ways in which the identified patient's symptoms are used for the maintenance of the family's preferred transactional system' and Dare's [28] 'the role of the family in minimising or amplifying the symptoms' are important strands in integrating the individual's and family's problems. Steinhauer [29,30,31], in his 'Process model of family functioning', took up this issue and showed how intrapersonal and interpersonal considerations can be linked. The model illuminates cases where individual and family therapy have been used and is probably particularly valuable if such an approach to treatment is adopted. It is to be noted that assessment and formulation not only give a basis for deciding on which treatment modalities are to be used, but also reveal in which areas the individual or family require help and give a basis for a preliminary decision on the details of treatment. Of course, as treatment proceeds, workers' understanding of the problems of the family should increase and the formulation and treatment plans will need continual revision.

So far, the need for assessment before deciding on choice of treatment has been spoken about as if there was a body of agreed knowledge from which a decision clearly follows. This is, unfortunately, not the case much of the time as regards the choice between family therapy and individual treatment with or without some involvement of the family. As regards indications and contra-indications for family therapy, different therapists and different schools of therapy hold widely different, even contradictory views, ranging from seeing family therapy as of almost universal application to seeing it as the treatment of last resort [32]. The issue is further complicated by different therapists stating their views in different ways.

In the light of the limited firm evidence on which decisions can be based about suitability for different forms of treatment and the lack of agreement among workers about indications and contra-indications, how can a worker arrive at a decision about treatment? When the problem is presented in relationship terms the decision will usually be for family or marital therapy, even when another family member has been blamed. Of course, there are times when one is presented with a relationship difficulty which is found to be attributable to an individual problem and this must be attended to. When the problem is presented as an individual one, the assessment, diagnosis and formulation should enable the worker to decide on the nature of the relationship of the individual symptomatology to disturbed family relationships. The decision about this gives some strong pointers as regards choice of treatment. Although the individual's symptomatology often relates to the disturbed family relationship in more than one of the ways described, the implications as regards choice of treatment will be considered first of all as if only one was possible at a time:

(a) As an expression of the family's dysfunction. Family therapy is the treatment of choice.

(b) Primary part of the problem with identified patient. Treatment for the underlying condition, if possible, is required. Family therapy may be appropriate for the family, both to help the family with its distress and to improve the outlook for the patient.

(c) Problem originally arose from disturbed family relationships but the identified patient now has problems in his own right. This is, in many ways, the most complex. With children and adolescents, these cases, however, do require involvement of the family (or other psycho-social system when not living at home) in treatment. In some cases when the problems are not too severe or too entrenched, work with the family alone may be sufficient. The nature of the work with the family may vary from individual or group counselling or psychotherapy for one or both parents, to family members, usually parents, being co-therapists in behaviour therapy, to family therapy. When it appears that the functioning of the family as a whole can be improved in this way and that the identified patient will improve in the less dysfunctional family system, family therapy is indicated. Family therapy may then also serve to reduce distress and pressure in the family while that improvement occurs. When the child is more disturbed or the problems more entrenched, he is likely to require some form of treatment in his own right. Work with the family in one of the ways described above will still be necessary and the reasons for the use of family therapy remain broadly the same. When there is doubt as to whether individual treatment will be required, it is quite often reasonable to commence with family therapy only.

(d) The identified patient as messenger. When a child or adolescent is sent as messenger to get help for the family as a whole, or for some part of the family, family therapy is indicated, particularly initially. Sometimes, once there has been some involvement with the family, it may emerge that treatment for another family member or another subsystem is necessary as the main thrust of treatment, usually combined with continuing family sessions. As has been mentioned, individual symptomatology is frequently linked to the disturbed family relationships in more than one way. In general, what is then required is a combination of the treatment approaches for each separately.

Are all the statements about indications and contra-indications for family therapy of any value [18,22,30,32,33,34,35,36]? The writer would suggest that they can be profitably used as aids when a decision on treatment is difficult, and as checks which should lead to reconsideration and discussion with colleagues when the worker finds that he is planning to take on for family therapy an individual and family who might be seen by other workers as unsuitable. In using statements about indications and contra-indications for family therapy in this way, it is important that the worker checks what sort of family therapy is being talked about. As Sue Walrond Skinner [32] points out, a contra-indication for one family therapy approach may be an indication for another. The question of availability of competent therapists for different approaches has already been touched on. The few well-controlled outcome studies too, particularly when they give a picture of the nature of the family therapy, have to be given particular attention. Indications and contra-indications should be similarly considered in regard to individual treatment and other forms of treatment.

It is likely to remain the case that each worker, depending on his skills, experience, theoretical viewpoint, personality and the support available to him, will establish his own view of how families can best be helped and how he can best work with a particular family. However, if progress is to be made, it is essential that, as the value of each treatment (including different methods of family therapy) becomes clearer, choice of treatment is made on the merits of the case. Steps will need to be taken to ensure that workers are trained, so that, in any area, the full range of treatments is available.

References

1. Rutter, M. *Children of Sick Parents: An Environmental and Psychiatric Study*. Institute of Psychiatry, Maudsley Monograph No.16, Oxford University Press, London, 1966.

2. Finer, M. *Report of the Committee on One-Parent Families*. H.M.S.O., London, 1974.

3. Framo, J.L. 'Marriage Therapy in a Couples Group'. In Bloch, D.A. (Ed.) *Techniques of Family Psychotherapy*. Grune & Stratton Inc., New York, 1973, 87-97.

4. Lahn, J.H. 'Communication with Children and Parents' *British Medical Journal*. 3, 1972, 406-408. (Also in *Emotional Problems of Childhood and Adolescence*. British Medical Association, London, 42-49.)

5. Balint, M. 'The Doctor's Therapeutic Function' *The Lancet*. 7397, 1965, 1177-1180.

6. Kanner, L. *Child Psychiatry* (3rd edition). Charles C. Thomas, Springfield, Illinois, 1957.

7. Hawton, K. & Blackstock, E. 'General Practice Aspects of Self-Poisoning and Self-Injury' *Psychological Medicine*. 6, 1976, 571-575.

8. Kempe, C.H. 'Paediatric Implications of the Battered Baby Syndrome' *Archives of Disease in Childhood*. 46, 1971, 28-37.

9. Corbett, J.A. 'Mental Retardation: Psychiatric Aspects'. In Rutter, M. & Hersov, L. (Eds.) *Child and Adolescent Psychiatry: Modern Approaches* (2nd edition). Blackwell Scientific Publications, 1985.

10. Leff, J.P., Kuipers, L., Berkowitz, R., Eberlein-Vries, R. & Sturgeon, D. 'A Controlled Trial of Social Intervention in the Families of Schizophrenic Patients' *British Journal of Psychiatry*. 141, 1982, 121-134.

11. Berkowitz, R. 'Therapeutic Intervention with Schizophrenic Patients and their Families: A Description of a Clinical Research Project' *Journal of Family Therapy*. 6, 3, 1984, 211-234.

12. Bowlby, J. 'The Making and Breaking of Affectional Bonds' *British Journal of Psychiatry*. 130, 1977, 421-431.

13. Axline, V.M. 'Play Therapy Procedures and Results' *American Journal of Orthopsychiatry*. 25, 1955, 619-626.

14. Axline, V.M. *DIBS: In Search of Self*. Penguin, Harmondsworth, 1971.

15. Slavson, S.R. & Schiffer, M. *Group Psychotherapies for Children*. International Universities Press Inc., New York, 1975.

16. Douglas, J. 'Behavioural Family Therapy and the Influence of a Systems Framework' *Journal of Family Therapy*. 3, 4, 1981, 327-339.

17. Frude, N. "The Family' and Psychotherapy'. In WalrondSkinner, S. (Ed.) *Psychotherapy: a Critical Approach*. Routledge & Kegan Paul, London, 1979, 14-44.

18. Walrond-Skinner, S. *Family Therapy – the Treatment of Natural Systems*. Routledge & Kegan Paul, London, 1976.

19. Satir, V. *Conjoint Family Therapy* (Revised edition). Science and Behavioural Books Inc., Palo Alto, California, 1967.

20. Minuchin, S. *Families and Family Therapy*. Tavistock Publications Ltd, London, 1974.

21. Haldane, I.J., Alexander, D.A. & Walker, L.G. *Models for Psychotherapy*. The University Press, Aberdeen, 1982.

22. Evans, J. *Adolescent and Pre-Adolescent Psychiatry*. Academic Press, London, 1982.

23. Fisher, L. 'On the Classification of Families' *Archives of General Psychiatry*. 34, 1977, 424-433.

24. Cox, A. & Rutter, M. 'Diagnostic Appraisal and Interviewing'. In Rutter, M. & Hersov L. (Eds.) *Child and Adolescent Psychiatry: Modern Approaches* (2nd edition). Blackwell Scientific Publications, 1985, 233-248.

25. Dare, C. 'Psychoanalysis and Systems in Family Therapy' *Journal of Family Therapy*. 1, 1979, 137-152.

26. Pincus, L. & Dare, C. *Secrets in the Family*. Faber and Faber, London, 1978.

27. Lieberman, S. 'Transgenerational Analysis: the Geneogram as a Technique in Family Therapy' *Journal of Family Therapy*. 1, 1, 1979, 51-64.

28. Dare, C. 'Family Therapy'. In Rutter, M. & Hersov, L. (Eds.) *Child and Adolescent Psychiatry: Modern Approaches* (2nd edition). Blackwell Scientific Publications, 1985, 809-825.

29. Steinhauer, P.D., Santabarbara, J. & Skinner H. 'The Process Model of Family Functioning' *Canadian Journal of Psychiatry*. 29, 1984, 77-88.

30. Steinhauer, P.D. & Tisdall, G.S. 'The Integrated Use of Individual and Family Psychotherapy' *Canadian Journal of Psychiatry*. 29, 1984, 89-97.

31. Steinhauer, P.D. 'Clinical Applications of the Process Model of Family Functioning' *Canadian Journal of Psychiatry*. 29, 1984, 98-111.

32. Walrond-Skinner, S. 'Indications and Contra-Indications for the Use of Family Therapy' *Journal of Child Psychology and Psychiatry*. 19, 1, 1978, 57-62.

33. Bloch, D.A. & Laperriere, K. 'Techniques of Family Therapy: a Conceptual Frame'. In Bloch, D.A. (Ed.) *Techniques of Family Psychotherapy*. Grune & Stratton Inc., New York, 1973, 1-19.

34. Elton, A. 'Indications for Selecting Family or Individual Therapy' *Journal of Family Therapy*. 1, 2, 1979, 193-201.

35. Offer, D. & Vanderstroer, E. 'Indications and Contraindications for Family Therapy'. In Feinstein, S.C. & Giouacchini, P. (Eds.) *Adolescent Psychiatry, Vol. III, Developmental and Clinical Studies*. Basic Books, New York, 1974, 249-262.

36. Skynner, A.C.R. *One Flesh: Separate Persons*. Constable, London, 1976, 223-246.

Methods of Social Work Practice with Families

Linda Hunt*

INTRODUCTION

The development of practice theory and, therefore, of methods and techniques for intervening purposefully in families experiencing difficulties, is dependent on the state of knowledge about the family. This collection of papers confirms what others (e.g. [1,2,3]) have said – that no coherent body of theory about the family yet exists and that in spite of the knowledge that has been accumulated through research, clinical experience and literature, we have no science of personal relationships. Different perspectives on the family have been pursued in different social disciplines. Sociology has focussed on the family as an institution and has examined its relationship with some other social institutions. Anthropology has paid particular attention to marriage patterns and is beginning to examine the impact of living in Britain on the traditional life-styles of minority families [4]. The study of relationships between marital partners and between parents and children has been pursued by clinical, social and developmental psychologists, but neither behavioural nor psycho-analytic schools of thought have so far provided an adequate theory of relationships [3].

The work that has been undertaken in the various disciplines does demonstrate that the family is a complex and varied phenomenon which poses problems for researchers. The definition of 'family', the diversity of family relationships, the very intimate and emotional nature of family life, the influence of societal norms on the way the family is conceptualised, are all problematic [5] and help to explain the slow rate of progress in developing and testing theoretical frameworks for understanding the family. Social work with families,

*It should be noted that the views expressed in this chapter cannot be assumed to reflect Scottish Office policy.

therefore, requires practitioners to move into a field, aspects of which are little understood. Yet social workers expect and are expected to act purposefully in their contacts with families. The practice theory they have developed to help them to do so has frequently been derived from experience, rather than from research findings or factual information [6]. Thus, it is rooted in a kind of pre-scientific 'folk' knowledge. It is often referred to as intuition. It is possible that this 'theory' may have validity, but it has not been validated. Quite properly, writers have tried to use the concepts and theoretical models of other disciplines to help them with the task. For example, standard texts like that of Hollis [7] and the review of approaches to casework edited by Roberts and Nee [8] demonstrate the extent to which psychoanalytic theory has been used to describe social work practice. There are, however, three serious constraints on this approach to developing practice theory. Firstly, it has relied on largely untested conceptual explanations of behaviour. Secondly, while subsequent practice experience suggests the models of intervention that authors describe may sometimes be helpful to clients, studies which establish the circumstances in which they can be expected to be effective have not been carried out. Thirdly, the tendency has been to behave as though the models are universally applicable and relevant and to ignore the fact that they are written from a particular socio-cultural perspective and consequently fixed in time and place.

These difficulties have sometimes prompted social workers consciously to reject attempts to develop theoretical frameworks for practice altogether. These practitioners concentrate on the unique qualities of each individual client (thereby implying that it is impossible to discover theory that has any general application) and rely on their spontaneous, intuitive responses to guide their practice [9]. Research carried out by Curnock and Hardiker [10] and by Sainsbury [11] has shown that some practitioners do make use of social work texts, but that they do this haphazardly, sometimes without being conscious of it and usually without thinking out how concepts fit with other elements of their model(s) of practice. Stevenson [12] describes these ways of working as being anti-intellectual and antipathetic to knowledge-building. She has suggested that they are common among social workers and their managers and that the comparative paucity of research by social work educators has helped to maintain this unsatisfactory situation (p. 23). It also seems probable that concentration on the features of each individual referral and avoiding methodical thinking through of the interventions being made, are means which social workers use to try to cope with the bewildering diversity of ideology and purpose that is such a significant feature of practice in local authority departments [13]. Unfortunately they are not satisfactory ways of coping, since they do nothing to help resolve the problems posed by diversity.

The kind of practice theory that social work most urgently needs to develop and test now is, as Lee[14] has pointed out, that which *begins* with and builds from the theories and findings emerging in the social science disciplines. What is required is the study of these 'theories of practice' [15], examination of their relevance to social work, the development of methods of intervention through which they can be applied and evaluation of the effects of applying them. This approach has the advantage that it encourages the testing and refinement of both the theoretical models and the practice itself. In addition, it does not deny practice wisdom and intuition, but rather acknowledges they exist and tries to make sure the components of them are made explicit and can be understood in theoretical, conceptual terms and tested. Practice theory of this type has begun to emerge over the last 20 years.

PRACTICE THEORY

In a thoughtful examination of styles of intervention designed to help people resolve problems in their personal relationships, Duck[16] points out that research has tended to concentrate on global characteristics and that practitioners apply methods of work as if all relationship problems are similar and can be similarly treated. Some of the disadvantages of the tendency to over-generalisation have been apparent for some time[17,18] and social workers using behavioural methods (e.g. [19,20]) have helped to make plain the positive advantages of establishing specific, achievable changes to which both client(s) and workers are committed. However, scholars have warned that research findings have not yet fully demonstrated what are the critical factors determining the success of an intervention (e.g. [21,22]), and evaluation of social skills training (a method in which specific goals *are* established) has shown that this method is not equally effective with all clients who demonstrate skill deficits in their personal relationships[23]. Clearly there are other significant influences on the outcome of interventions.

One of these is the nature of the difficulty experienced by the family. It can be demonstrated that every relationship is a complex of independently developing features and that relationships deteriorate at many different levels and in many different ways. It can be predicted that outcome will be affected by the practitioner's ability to match the method of intervention with the particular type of problem a family is experiencing. However, although a number of ways of conceptualising interaction within relationships have been developed, little progress has been made in testing their validity[24]. We know little about the external factors which influence breakdown, or about what are the distinctive patterns of behaviour which characterise disturbed families. Consequently, it is not possible for the practitioner to identify reliably the nature and stage of the family problems presented to him/her or to be certain about the appropriate match between method and goals. In this unsatisfactory situation there are three things which can help practitioners.

1. Empathy and Commitment

It is likely that practitioners' ability to identify the central issues will be increased if they can elicit, understand and demonstrate appreciation of family members' experience and perception of what is happening: in other words, if they are empathic in their early contact with family members and demonstrate commitment to being helpful. It is now possible to identify the components of practitioner behaviour which constitute therapeutic commitment and an empathic approach to clients [25,26]. Research indicates that in some situations at least it is the practitioner's capacity for empathy that is the most significant factor influencing successful outcome [27,28,29]. The descriptions of initial contact written by behavioural social workers (e.g. [21]), by family therapists of a variety of perspectives (e.g. [30,31,32]), by practitioners in family centres [33] and others interested in networking and community social work, all directly or implicitly emphasise the importance of beginning with the family's perception of what is wrong.

Although few mention empathy and therapeutic commitment, or fully discuss their components, it is clear they assume a committed, empathic approach to be critically important. However, experience teaches that prejudice and preconceptions are regularly imported into contacts with clients. Mattinson and Sinclair [34] suggest that the priorities and intake structures, that have been introduced in some local authority area teams, may so limit the range of factors and possibilities taken into account that critical aspects of clients' problem situations are excluded from consideration; and it is vividly clear that preconceptions about assimilation and about the issues that concern minority families have inhibited capacity to understand and respond to the experience of those families [4,35,36]. Re-examination of the components of empathy and commitment, and attention to the development of skills associated with these, are tasks with high priority if practitioners are to maximise their capacity to be effective.

2. Frameworks to Assist Problem Analysis

Two conceptual frameworks which focus on problem analysis seem particularly helpful.

(a) General Systems Theory [37] outlined a framework for understanding 'the organismic features of life, behaviour, society', and out of this there emerged a way of analysing situations which enabled practitioners to take account of the 'entire range of elements that bear on a social problem – including the social units involved, their expansive and dynamic characteristics and inter-relations and the implications of change in one as it affects all others' (p. 110) [6]. The impact of the theory has been profound. It has been taken into the thinking of psycho-analysts working with families [38]; it has influenced the development of theory in psychology [16]; and it has been absorbed and developed in sociology and in management sciences [39,40].

Significance had always been accorded to the client's family and social network by social workers, but by holding them in mind rather than through seeking their active involvement in problem resolution. Although a few practitioners had begun working jointly with married couples [41] and occasionally with teenagers and their parents in the 1960s, individual casework continued to be the main approach to work with families. Later, pressure to acknowledge the significance of interaction between family members encouraged attempts to work with nuclear family groups, using ideas developed in child psychiatry [30,42]. By this time the generality of social workers were becoming increasingly aware that changes were taking place in the characteristic structures of families, that the concept of the family held by people whose traditions were in countries such as Jamaica or India was significantly different from their own, that the role and status of women was changing and that all these issues were reflected in the family problems referred to them. Social workers were also beginning to consider the social network as a resource which could be mobilised to assist the resolution of family problems and to enable families to cope with stress and illness. The social work profession really needed a means of bringing all these developments together in a way which helped practitioners to make decisions about where and how to intervene. The systems approach seemed to offer this. Once developed [6,43,44] it was rapidly taken into methods teaching on qualifying courses.

The systems approach to problem analysis confirmed what had already emerged from small group theory [45,46]: that personal pathology and linear causality were quite inadequate approaches to analysing and responding to problems. It helped to make it plain that some problems do lie within an individual 'identified client', but that the locus of most problems lies elsewhere – in sub-groups within a family, within the nuclear family, in the relationships within the extended family, in relationships between a family and other formal (e.g. school, D.H.S.S., Housing Department, employers) and informal (neighbourhood, peer groups) organisations and in the relationship between families and the wider socio-political structure. When this was put together with findings emerging from group work about the power and significance of the help group members give to each other, and about the way in which the interaction between group members can provide both a demonstration of the problems people are experiencing and a means of attempting problem resolution, a radical change in thinking and practice became possible[47].

At times too great claims were made for systems theory: at first some seemed to regard it as a universally applicable method of intervention. Later, it was recognised to be a way of understanding situations. As such it offers the possibility of dealing with the tension between the individual focus and socio-political focus that has been apparent in social work, by giving proper emphasis to both, rather than by rejecting one in favour of the other as tended to occur in the past[48,49]. It enables decisions to be made about which issues will be the focus of work and encourages clients and practitioners to establish explicit goals. Far from advocating one particular method, it increases awareness of the fact that problems which emerge in families are of different types and require a whole repertoire of methods and techniques for their resolution[50]. It is at least in part a consequence of the application of systems thinking that a new range of ways of working with families is emerging. The different styles of family therapy, the work undertaken in family centres[51,52], the concept of community social workers[53], the patch system of working[54,55], networking[56,57] and the ecological model of practice[58] are all to some degree grounded in systems theory.

Research in Britain suggests that in spite of the impact of systems thinking, individual casework has continued to be the approach most frequently used by social workers[9,10,59]. This should be neither a surprise nor a disappointment. It has been estimated, for example, that the time lag between the publication of relevant theory, research and experimental practice applications and their absorption into the practice of the generality of professionals concerned with alcohol problems may be 20 years[60] and there is no reason to suppose that change can be achieved more quickly in social work practice. Work recently carried out in the Central Advisory Service of Social Work Services Group[61,62,63] certainly seems to confirm that practitioners in many agencies know about systems theory and provides evidence that some are using a systems approach to help them identify the nature and locus of the family problems.

(b) Work carried out by a number of psychologists in the last few years has concentrated on the development and dissolution of personal relationships [64,65,66]. This has included attempts to review what is known about attraction, satisfaction and breakdown in relationships and is particularly useful for the attempt Duck [16] makes to analyse the process through which marital relationships progress from the emergence of a problem to decline, breakdown and dissolution. He first points out the importance of recognising that some problems do not start with the relationship: they pre-date it. Some people have little capacity to create trusting, intimate relationships and will be unable to sustain a satisfying marital partnership. If these people are to achieve greater satisfaction and stability in their relationships, the focus of intervention has to be on repair and development of their skills and capacities. It is intrapersonal rather than interpersonal issues that should be the initial focus. The detailed study Mattinson and Sinclair [34] carried out in a local authority area team suggests one method of working with these clients. It also seems likely they might be helped by individual casework since, as Sainsbury's [11] study of 27 families in contact with a Family Service Unit found, casework does seem to be helpful in promoting improvement in self esteem and other self-related feelings.

Duck goes on to describe the process of the dissolution of (marital) relationships as containing five phases, pointing out that the critical issues of each phase seem to be different and to require different responses from helping agents. The practical utility of his analysis is clear. If he has correctly defined the phases and their specific characteristics, the possibility of achieving an appropriate match between goals and methods of intervention will be enhanced. Furthermore, although his analysis has not been fully confirmed by research, it is presented in a form which should allow practitioners to test its validity in practice.

3. A Repertoire of Methods of Intervention

The third aid to the practitioner is implicit in the discussion of empathy and of the two frameworks for analysing the type, locus and form of problems presented by families. It is the availability to the social worker of a repertoire of methods and techniques. One method or set of techniques cannot usefully be applied to all family problems. The practitioner needs to be able consciously to select from a range of ways of working, to apply a specific approach that seems well matched to the purpose of the intervention, to evaluate its effectiveness and to be ready to abandon it for another if it does not work. This last point is very important. The tendency in social work has been to conclude that if a method of work is not effective it should be applied with greater intensity. However, research findings indicate that applying more of the same cannot be assumed to lead to an increase in successful outcomes [67,68]. If a method proves ineffective in achieving the desired changes it is important to review why this may be so and to consider whether a different way of working may hold more promise. It seems probable that a practitioner who is unable to try out alternative solutions to a problem is unlikely to be able to help family members to discover new patterns of interaction. A practitioner cannot, of course, become equally competent across the entire range. Each practitioner will have to select from the range, but a team of social workers can be expected to offer skills across a wider spectrum.

The discussion which follows examines relevant factors to be taken into account when making a decision about how to intervene constructively and reviews some methods of work that might be employed.

MARITAL DIFFICULTIES

The phases of breakdown in marital relationships identified by Duck [16] can be used to help identify ways of working. The process towards dissolution is identified as beginning with a situation in which the relationship is experienced as less rewarding than formerly. At this stage the person still demonstrates basic acceptance of the partner. The concern is with lack of satisfaction rather than dislike; an improvement in the content of the partnership is most likely to be helpful, therefore. The goals of intervention should be improved communication between partners, re-establishing attractiveness within the relationship and increasing intimacy. Joint work with the partners that enables them to increase their understanding of what is going on will be the first task; that should be followed by interventions designed to achieve specific changes in behaviour and interaction. The couple's stage in the family life cycle and their socio-cultural expectations of marriage will be influences on the focus of attention. For example, the birth of children seems to be associated with decline in marital satisfaction, especially for women [69], and one research study suggests that no matter what a family's socio-economic circumstance the least satisfactory period of marriage for women is when the family contains school age children [70]. Family life is often experienced as a solitary burden for women at this stage. Having a sense of cohesion and concerned and committed involvement in a joint enterprise are the factors that seems most likely to alleviate this dissatisfaction [70,71]. A small group of parents whose children are on the 'at risk' register in one part of Scotland recently expressed exactly this view to me.

Interventive techniques which focus attention on ways by which a couple can discover how to share responsibilities and which help partners to demonstrate to each other the value they place on the marital subsystem within the family, would be likely to help resolve difficulties.

Although research has demonstrated that conflict is a common feature of family life [72], partners generally have high expectations of romance and intimacy in marriage which may be especially difficult to approximate in contemporary Britain [24]. Greater mobility and the emphasis on the nuclear family make it possible for extended family bonds and ties with the social network to be weakened, while changes in the role and expectations of women disturb the traditional balance of many aspects of family life. These factors may be significant features of the second phase towards the dissolution of the partnership. Duck [16] suggests this is characterised by brooding and recrimination. One partner is already beginning to withdraw from the relationship, although residual attraction to it is also present. It is in this phase that the disaffected partner may seek help from a formal helping agency without the other's knowledge; the central question for the person is whether it would be justifiable to withdraw from the relationship altogether. The practitioner, trying to help the person to re-establish a more satisfactory relationship, will therefore focus first on the positive qualities of the *partner* and then examine what the *person* is contributing to the difficulties; later conjoint work with the partners will help them to identify and emphasise the positive qualities of their relationship. In the past, social workers have tended to encourage clients to express their negative feelings freely, believing it to be helpful in almost all circumstances for the practitioner to demonstrate the capacity to cope with these feelings and that clients would eventually talk their way out of negative positions. The work of behavioural psychologists has suggested, however, that ventilation may serve only to reinforce negative positions, that it may be more helpful to focus on the positive components of the situation and reframe issues so that they are described not in terms of problem behaviour but of desired behaviour [73]. It is suggested that emphasis on the negative aspects of the partner will not be constructive at this stage. It is likely to be more helpful for the person to be encouraged to try to understand the problematic behaviour of the partner and to attempt to make changes that will increase the possibility of achieving what is desired.

The person seeking help may conclude that the negative qualities of the partner are more significant than the advantages of remaining in the relationship. When this happens it will be necessary to change the focus of the intervention and the methods used, since the meaning of the relationship and the possible alternatives to it will become central issues. At this point the attitude of extended family and social networks may also become important, opening up questions for the practitioner about whether the preferred method of working with the problem is with the individual, the marital partners, or a larger family group. It isn't likely to be appropriate to consider working directly with the social network while the focus remains the repair of the marital relationship, although it may help to relieve the pressure on a distressed partner if key people in the network know that there is marital disharmony and an attempt to resolve it is being made.

The third phase of the dissolution begins with both partners acknowledging doubts about the continued existence of their relationship. Both will be uncertain about the possible outcome of confronting each other with their dissatisfaction; however, it is suggested that the expression of tension and hostility will be cathartic since it will reduce recrimination and it will help them to expose and explore the problem(s) rather than concentrate on the emotions which are its result. Behavioural and cognitive methods of working with the couple may be particularly useful once problems have been elicited and desired changes are agreed [74]. Although the central problem is within the marital relationship, it will often be apparent that the children of the partnership are affected by and involved in the process of interaction that has been established. Steinglass [75], for example, has constructed a series of hypotheses about how this may occur in families in which one marital partner has an alcohol problem. It will, therefore, be important to consider whether to concentrate on working with the couple or to invite the active participation of other members of the family. A systems approach to problem analysis will assist the practitioner in making a decision about this. Meetings which bring together the complete nuclear family may be the most useful and one of several models of family therapy might be used (e.g. [32,49,76]) or adapted. This last point is important. Knowledge about the different models is insufficient to demonstrate that there is a 'best approach' in any particular circumstance, so there can be no orthodoxy about family therapy practice as yet [77]. In addition it is clear that the statutory functions of probation and local authority departments and the authority which practitioners in those settings carry, mean that family therapy has to be adapted to take account of factors not present in the settings in which family therapy was first developed [78]. Analysis of what adaptation is required, and of the circumstances in which family therapy can be applied in those settings is beginning to emerge[79,80,81] and Manor[82] has edited a handbook which suggests what application and adaptation might mean in terms of practical action by the practitioner.

Bell[30] and behavioural social workers engaging in family work (e.g [21]) outline models of work that allow flexibility about which family members will be included in particular sessions. These open up the possibility of concentrating on the subsystem within the family which is central to the problem in focus. Thus the marital partners might meet with the practitioner to work on the resolution of their difficulties, while at another time the focus might shift to the repair of the parent-child relationship or to providing the children with the opportunity to work separately on the difficulties they experience as a consequence of their parents' problems (see below for further discussion).

The third phase of deterioration in the marital relationship brings the partners to a crossroads. The essential question is what form the relationship is to take in the future. The intervention is likely to be most helpful if it concentrates on changing patterns of activity and routine and working towards new levels of affection between partners. Clearly, long-established patterns of interaction will have been absorbed by the children of the couple and taken into account by other significant family members and change is unlikely to be achieved without their participation. (Work with the family as a whole is further discussed on p.149).

During the fourth phase of deterioration of the marital relationship one or both partners talk with friends and relatives about what is happening; they enlist allies and explore the social consequences of breaking up the relationship. It is still possible that difficulties can be resolved at this stage, though much may depend on the influence of the social network. Duck seems to suggest that partners may be less likely to seek the help of agencies at this stage unless there is real interest in repairing the relationship. The factors influencing a search for outside 'expert' help may be a little more complicated than this, however. Two interacting variables are likely to be at work in the situation:

1. The degree of congruence between the views of family and friends about what should happen and the wishes of the partners.

2. The authority and influence of the extended family on the partners.

Resistance by the family to the dissolution of the relationship, accompanied by a high degree of dependency on key relatives, seems likely to lead one or both partners to feel that the disadvantages expected to flow from the dissolution of the relationship would outweigh the advantages of release from an unsatisfactory partner. Though such a situation might be productive of a high level of stress, it would be hard for either partner to take an initiative to seek outside help. If family members and both partners are convinced the relationship should be ended there is little need for outside help, but if the family advocate dissolution while one or both partners want to try to repair their relationship, a request for external and more objective and expert help seems more likely.

Some couples whose relationship is at this stage in the process of breakdown and dissolution will already be known to social workers, frequently because of other problems which are related to marital disharmony, such as behavioural difficulties in one of the children. Family members may not be able to work purposefully in these situations unless the marital difficulties can become a focus of attention. There will be occasions, therefore, when the practitioner will wish to initiate discussion about the marital relationship, whether or not the couple has indicated a wish for this. This delicate work may be done best by means of family group or network meetings.

In the fourth phase of breakdown the couple may take the decision to dissolve their relationship. Each partner can be helped to adjust to this ending by his/her family and social network, and it will be useful if the practitioner assists the partners to mobilise the network(s). Some partners may discover their network has become inadequate for providing the support they want and need help in extending it and in discovering ways of developing their use of the resources it can provide [83,56]. Once dissolution has become the goal and the person feels it is justifiable to pursue it, the practitioner's task will be to assist its achievement in a way which allows the loss to be experienced and ensures that the sense of worth and self confidence of the people concerned is not altogether eclipsed. Jenkins' paper [77] explores relevant issues about loss and Marris' classic text [84] complements and enlarges this perspective. In this final phase, described by Duck as 'grave dressing', it is important for both partners to formulate a history of the relationship with which they can be comfortable and which will allow each to explore the possibility of developing other personal relationships in the future. Partners may require help with these tasks in individual interviews or they may wish to join self-help groups as individuals. There may be aspects of these tasks, however, which it is helpful to work on together or with other family members. It may be particularly important for the nuclear family to meet together when the couple have dependent children.

WORKING WITH FAMILY GROUPS

Discussion of modes of practice aimed at resolving difficulties whose locus is essentially within the marital relationship, has already brought to light a number of circumstances in which practice goals would seem to be best achieved through methods of intervention that involve the active participation of the whole family. There are very many other difficulties occurring within families for which such methods seem the most likely to provide a satisfactory solution. The collection of papers edited by Treacher and Carpenter [31] and Gorell Barnes' [85] introductory text provide an insight into the range of problems and the variety of settings in which this seems to be the case. The principal modes of working with the family as a whole are outlined in a collection of papers designed to help identify the differences and similarities between them and to make it easier to select appropriate treatment strategies [49], and Walrond-Skinner discusses some recent developments in thinking and practice [86].

The effectiveness of these models of working with the family has not been unequivocally demonstrated [24] but the available evidence does suggest they have value. There is some evidence to suggest that interventions based on behavioural principles may be the most effective [20,87], although this is to an extent challenged by Gurman and Kniskern [88]. Practitioners are using a variety of approaches to family therapy and some have enough experience of successful cases to give them confidence to be more systematic in their use and evaluation of the approaches (e.g. [89]). More small scale studies of the kind which can be undertaken by practitioners are necessary, if intervention strategies and techniques that show promise and can be tested in further practice are to be identified and developed.

The literature suggests that the significant feature common to all models of family therapy is that they require practitioners to structure their work: clarity about the precise responsibilities of the practitioner and of the family members is sought from the beginning (e.g. [90,20]); goals are agreed and contracts are made (e.g. [19,91]); time limits (not always short term) may be set (e.g. [92]). Through these and other techniques (e.g. homework tasks completed between family interviews) it seems to become easier for family members to understand what is happening and to commit themselves to participation in working to the agreed goals [93,85,89]. Wertheim [94] suggests that this happens because focussing and structuring the initial contacts with the family enables them to mobilise into constructive, ordered action (rather than into the chaotic disorder which is such a feature of many disturbed families) the constant energy for change which exists in everyone. The work of the Child Protection

Team of Rochdale NSPCC seems to confirm that this energy can be mobilised to good purpose by some of the most dangerous and difficult families referred [89,95]. Ainley [79] suggests that structure and the proper recognition and use of authority can be positively helpful aspects of family therapy practice with both adults and juveniles in the probation setting. Practitioners in many settings, who are applying family therapy techniques, are discovering that the authoritative use of structure and focus significantly enlarges family members' scope to decide whether or not they will join in, and what and when they are willing to contribute. As Gorell Barnes [85] says, families can be moved from experiencing themselves as passive victims of social forces to being people having some choice of action (p.29). This finding is consistent with the earlier work of Mayer and Timms [18] and Sainsbury [11], which highlighted the confusion and lack of purpose felt by a significant proportion of the clients in their studies, who had received casework help in which the goals had not been made clear and interviews lacked structure. Sainsbury recognised that the evidence of his study indicated that the exercise of authority was compatible with effective work and noted that members of five (out of 23) families actually said this was so.

The clarity about goals and tasks that emerges for both practitioners and family members has a number of additional advantages. It helps practitioners to choose the interventions that seem likely to be effective [91]; an atmosphere is created in which practitioners can be direct and explicit about what they will contribute and about the formal responsibilities they carry on behalf of their agencies; it makes it possible to establish what has to be changed and whether movement towards the required change is occurring [21]; the critical issues are shared with family members, making it easy for them actively to participate in the review of goals and progress.

The available models of family therapy have, then, a number of aspects that suggest they can usefully be applied whenever problem analysis indicates that family involvement will be critical to problem resolution. As has already been noted, there are cases of non-accidental injury to children where family therapy seems to be effective. The recent British literature on work with families also suggests it can be used to help resolve a variety of other child-care problems. Some behavioural social workers are taking a more radical line and proposing that instead of working directly with parents and children, the practitioner should teach parents the techniques that will enable problem behaviours in children to be extinguished and provide consultation and support to parents while they apply these techniques [96]. Problems associated with mental illness often affect the nuclear family as a whole and although research has so far not adequately demonstrated the dynamics of interaction between family life and mental illness or what changes to the situation are critical[97], the application of family therapy and a family-oriented approach to psychiatric emergencies has proved useful in some instances[98,78,99]. The discussion by Rack[100], of ways in which cultural factors affect mental illness and the relationship with psychiatric services among people from the Indian sub-continent now settled in Britain, suggests that the participation of the nuclear family and key members of the extended family in problem resolution may also be necessary for at least some ethnic minority families. Alcohol problems are family problems too, and a number of circumstances can be justified when it will be important to involve family members in problem resolution[101]. Steinglass'[75] analysis of roles and problem maintenance in families where one member has an alcohol problem, is helpful in suggesting where intervention and change is needed, while Anderson and Henderson[102] provide a description of family therapy practice where drinking behaviour is central and Cork[103] and Wilson[104] identify the importance to some of the children of these families of separate individual contact with the practitioner.

This very brief outline gives an indication of the range of situations in which direct involvement of family members can be useful. It should be noted that the use of family therapy does not preclude the use of other methods and techniques. For example, the concepts and techniques of crisis intervention[105,106] remain useful in psychiatric emergencies whether or not the practitioner chooses to convene a family meeting. Family therapy is no panacea; individual counselling, group activities and other resources will be required to meet some family problems.

FAMILY AND SOCIAL NETWORK

The importance of providing a range of resources to families has been well recognised by practitioners involved in the development of family centres[52] and by some trying to develop community social work practice (e.g. the Family Groups Project (COPE) described in Hadley et al.[107]). Successful family centres certainly provide structure and encourage families to focus on specific achievable goals, but they offer a wider range of facilities and opportunities to address a greater variety of concerns than the models of family work already discussed. Family centres offer opportunities to develop parenting skills, play opportunities for deprived and handicapped children and health education programmes. They provide creative activities, welfare rights advice, scope for making friendships, personal and group counselling, family therapy and self-help activities. Their focus is on the involvement of the whole family and they also recognise the significance to families of the neighbourhood in which they live and the social network of which they are part. Elements of this approach are also now visible in some projects designed to provide services to families who belong to ethnic minority groups in Britain (e.g. [108 and 109]).

Baldock [110] has pointed out that although the local community may be spoken of as if it exists as a single entity, in fact it is the social networks of individuals and families that are tangible and can become active. These networks are not always contained within the geographic boundaries of what might be described as the local community. They are composed of relatives, friends, teachers, employers etc. as well as neighbours. There is evidence to suggest that active networks can be a significant resource to families and an influence upon them [111]. In fact, unrealistically optimistic predictions of the capacity of network members to provide help are apparent in some recent exhortations to develop 'community care'. As Unger and Powell [111] and Bayley [112] point out, the help that different elements of the network can provide tends to be situation-specific and it is necessary to discover what types of help it is realistic to expect from particular segments of the network. The information currently available about the range of services required indicates that formal helping agencies are likely to remain as necessary as the rest of the network to the well-being of many families, and that agency staff will be most effective if they develop links with networks and seek to provide complementary assistance. The tasks of identifying problems and developing the means of resolving them can then be conceptualised as a joint responsibility for the practitioner, the individual, his/her family and others in the social network [113]. This, it seems, is the perspective on which those working in family centres base their approach to practice. They have recognised that the networks of particular families are very small or may have ceased to be active, and have often provided opportunities and activities designed to increase the size of an individual's or a family's network and to make it easier for the components of the network to remain active. Their approach has usually been indirect – in contrast to other practitioners who are beginning to see 'networking' as a method of working with families.

Practitioners who are developing this method hold the view that networks are not only positive resources but that some problems require action in the social network for their resolution. In an interesting example of the application of the method, Waters et al. [114] describe the convening of network meetings attended by the family concerned and all the representatives of formal agencies involved with them. The authors argue that in some situations where practitioners become stuck and unable to provide constructive help to a family, the problem lies within the helping network and can only be resolved by it.

Since it began to be developed in the 1960s networking has been used in a wide range of settings and situations [56,115]. It is recognised that convening a network meeting requires skill and perseverance and that families may need help in learning how to elicit support and help from network members [116.] Networks are also recognised to have negative components and limited capacity for change [83,117], but these factors have themselves been used to argue for the use of the method in rural communities. Bagarozzi [118] suggests that only by involving key members of the neighbourhood network will it be possible in a rural community to change the position and status of individuals and families who have been categorised or stigmatised because of mental illness, delinquency or some other behaviour regarded as deviant. Only if change occurs in the attitudes and expectations of those around them, it is argued, will the individual and the family be given the scope to change their behaviour and position.

The introduction of a network-oriented service for elderly people has recently been described and advocated by a practitioner working in a psycho-geriatric unit [57]. Perhaps networking offers an effective means of developing the kind of community support that PSSRU studies have shown can be successful in enabling elderly people to remain in their own homes [119]. The method does seem to hold promise of being useful to a range of clients, and Brake [120] has suggested that professional training courses might teach a radical approach to practice which combines elements of family therapy with network intervention and addresses issues of power and political relatedness in family and social relations. Little research has so far been attempted, however, and it is not yet possible to be certain about the critical elements of this way of working or about which problems it is most likely to be effective in resolving.

CONCLUSION

Recent literature provides social work practitioners with a number of specific models for working with families and a considerable range of practical techniques that can be used to achieve change and the resolution of problems. These ways of working are built upon ideas and findings in other social sciences and are formulated and applied in ways which are beginning to make systematic evaluation more feasible. There is still little certainty about what makes social work intervention effective [17], but there are indicators that the introduction of structure, the identification, pursuit and review of specific goals and the matching of the method of intervention used to the problem(s) being addressed make successful outcome more likely. The development of greater certainty about what makes interventions effective, could be significantly assisted by a more systematic approach by practitioners to the evaluation of their work with families, and a willingness to share the results. Useful and reliable practice theory can only emerge if practitioners, thinkers and researchers all make their contributions.

References

1. Handel, J. (Ed.) *The Psycho-social Interior of the Family* (3rd edition). Aldine, New York, 1985.
2. Hinde, R. *Towards Understanding Relationships*. Academic Press, London, 1979.
3. Hinde, R. 'The Bases of a Science of Personal Relationships'. In Duck, S. and Gilmour, R. (Eds.) *Studying Personal Relationships* (Personal Relationships 1). Academic Press, London, 1981.
4. Khan, V. (Ed.) *Minority Families in Britain*. Macmillan, London, 1979.
5. McCarthy, B. 'Studying Personal Relationships'. In Duck, S. and Gilmour, R. (Eds.) *Studying Personal Relationships* (Personal Relationships 1). Academic Press, London, 1981.
6. Goldstein, H. *Social Work Practice: A Unitary Approach*. University of South Carolina, 1973.
7. Hollis, F. *Casework: a Psychosocial Therapy*. Random House Publications, New York, 1964.
8. Roberts, R. & Nee, R. (Eds.) *Theories of Social Casework*. Chicago University Press, 1970.
9. Stevenson, O. & Parsloe, P. *Social Service Teams: The Practitioners' View*. H.M.S.O., London, 1978.
10. Curnock, K. & Hardiker, P. *Towards Practice Theory*. Routledge and Kegan Paul, London, 1979.
11. Sainsbury, E. *Social Work with Families*. Routledge and Kegan Paul, London, 1975.
12. Stevenson, O. *Specialisation in Social Service Teams*. Allen & Unwin, London, 1981.
13. Sainsbury, E. 'Diversity in Social Work Practice: an Overview of the Problem' *Issues in Social Work Education*. 5, 1, 1985, 3-12.
14. Lee, P. 'Some Contemporary and Perennial Problems of Relating Theory to Practice in Social Work'. In Bailey, R. and Lee, P. (Eds.) *Theory and Practice in Social Work*. Blackwell, Oxford, 1982.
15. Evans, R. 'Some Implications of an Integrated Model for Social Work Theory and Practice' *British Journal of Social Work*. 6, 2, 1976, 177-200.
16. Duck, S. 'A Perspective on the Repair of Personal Relationships'. In Duck, S. (Ed.) *Repairing Personal Relationships* (Personal Relationships 5). Academic Press, London, 1984.

17. Goldberg, E. & Connolly, N. 'Postscript'. In Goldberg, E. & Connolly, N. (Eds.) *Evaluative Research in Social Care*. Heinemann, London, 1981.

18. Mayer, J. & Timms, N. *The Client Speaks: Working Class Impressions of Casework*. Routledge and Kegan Paul, London, 1970.

19. Stein, T. & Gambrill, E. 'Contracts in Foster Care'. In Schinke, S. (Ed.) *Behavioural Methods in Social Welfare*. Aldine Press, New York, 1981.

20. Pinkston, E., Levitt, J., Green, G. et al. *Effective Social Work Practice*. Jossey-Bass, London, 1982.

21. Gambrill, E. 'A Behavioural Perspective of Families'. In Tolson, E. & Reid, W. (Eds.) *Models of Family Treatment*. Columbia University Press, New York, 1981.

22. Reid, W. & Hanrahan, P. 'The Effectiveness of Social Work: Recent Evidence'. In Goldberg, E. & Connolly, N. (Eds.) *Evaluative Research in Social Care*. Heinemann, London, 1981.

23. Trower, P. 'Social Skill Disorder'. In Ducks, S. & Gilmour, R. (Eds.) *Personal Relationships in Disorder* (Personal Relationships 3). Academic Press, London, 1981.

24. Orford, J. & O'Reilly, P. 'Disorders in the Family'. In Duck, S. & Gilmour, R. (Eds.) *Personal Relationships in Disorder* (Personal Relationships 3). Academic Press, London, 1981.

25. Kiesler, D. et al. 'A Summary of Issues and Conclusions'. In Rogers, C. (Ed.) *The Therapeutic Relationship and its Impact*. Wisconsin Press, 1967.

26. Cartwright, A. 'Are Different Therapeutic Perspectives Important in the Treatment of Alcoholism?' *British Journal of Addictions*. 76, 1981, 347-361.

27. Miller, W., Taylor, C. et al. 'Focused versus Broad Spectrum Behaviour Therapy for Problem Drinkers' *Journal of Consulting and Clinical Psychology*. 48, 5, 1980, 590-601.

28. Kniskern, D. & Gurman, A. 'Research on Training in Marriage and Family Therapy' *Journal of Marriage and Family Therapy*. 5, 1979, 469-474.

29. Cartwright, A. 'Is Treatment an Effective Way of Helping Clients Resolve their Difficulties with Alcohol?' (unpublished paper). 1984.

30. Bell, J. 'The Small Group Perspective: Family Group Therapy'. In Tolson, E. & Reid, W. (Eds.) *Models of Family Treatment*. Columbia University Press, New York, 1981.

31. Treacher, A. & Carpenter, J. (Eds.) *Using Family Therapy*. Blackwell, Oxford, 1984.

32. Walrond-Skinner, S. *Family Therapy: The Treatment of Natural Systems*. Routledge and Kegan Paul, London, 1976.

33. Adamson, J. & Warren, C. *Welcome to St. Gabriel's Family Centre*. The Children's Society, London, 1983.

34. Mattinson, J. & Sinclair, J. *Mate and Stalemate*. Blackwell, Oxford, 1979.

35. Cheetham, J. (Ed.) *Social Work and Ethnicity*. Allen and Unwin, London, 1982.

36. Ellis, J. (Ed.) *West African Families in Britain*. Routledge and Kegan Paul, London, 1978.

37. von Bertalanffy *General Systems Theory*. Penguin, Harmondsworth, 1971.

38. Yelloly, M. *Social Work Theory and Psychoanalysis*. Van Nostrand and Reinhold, Wokingham, 1980.

39. Lawrence, G. (Ed.) *Exploring Individual and Organisational Boundaries*. Wiley, London, 1979.

40. Beishon, R. & Peters, G. (Eds.) *Systems Behaviour*. Open University Press, London, 1981.

41. Family Discussion Bureau. *The Marital Relationship as a Focus for Casework*. Codicote Press, London, 1962.

42. Bell, J. *Family Group Therapy*. Bookstall Publications, London, 1969.

43. Pincus, A. & Minahan, A. *Social Work Practice: Model and Method*. F.E. Peacock, Illinois, 1973.

44. Vickery, A. 'A Systems Approach to Social Work Intervention' *British Journal of Social Work*. 4,4, 1974, 389-404.

45. Cartwright, D. & Zander, A. (Eds.) *Group Dynamics: Research and Theory*. Harper Row, New York, 1960.

46. Bion, W. *Experiences in Groups*. Tavistock Publications, London, 1961.

47. Sherman, S. 'A Social Work Frame for Family Therapy'. In Tolson, E. & Reid, W. (Eds.) *Models of Family Treatment*. Columbia University Press, New York, 1981.

48. Loewenberg, F. *Fundamentals of Social Intervention* (2nd edition). Columbia University Press, New York, 1983.

49. Tolson, E. & Reid, W. *Models of Family Treatment*. Columbia University Press, New York, 1981.

50. Holder, D. & Wardle, M. *Teamwork and the Development of a Unitary Approach*. Routledge and Kegan Paul, London, 1981.

51. Phelan, J. *Family Centres: A Study*. The Children's Society, London, 1983.

52. Adamson, J. & Warren, C. 'Family Centres'. In Walton, R. et al. (in preparation).

53. Barclay Report. *Social Workers, their Roles and Tasks*. Bedford Square Press, London, 1982.

54. Sinclair, I. & Thomas, D. *Perspectives on Patch*. NISW, London, 1983.

55. Hadley, R. & McGrath, M. *Going Local: Neighbourhood Social Services*. Bedford Square Press, London, 1980.

56. Rueveni, V. *Networking Families in Crisis*. Human Sciences Press, New York, 1979.

57. Pottle, S. 'Network oriented Service for the Elderly'. In Treacher, A. & Carpenter, J. (Eds.) *Using Family Therapy*. Blackwell, Oxford, 1984.

58. Germain, C. (Ed.) *Social Work Practice: People and Environments, An Ecological Perspective*. Columbia University Press, New York, 1979.

59. Sainsbury, E., Nixon, S. & Phillips, D. *Social Work in Focus*. Routledge and Kegan Paul, London, 1982.

60. Walsh, D. *Alcohol-Related Medico-Social Problems and their Prevention*. World Health Organisation, Geneva, 1982.

61. Central Advisory Service. *Social Work Practice in Long-term Cases*. SWSG, Edinburgh (in preparation).

62. Central Advisory Service. *Practitioners' Use of Methods of Intervention* (unpublished paper).

63. Central Advisory Service. *The Application of Family Therapy in Local Authority Social Work Departments*. SWSG (in preparation).

64. Duck, S. & Gilmour, R. (Eds.) *Studying Personal Relationships* (Personal Relationships 1). Academic Press, London, 1981a.

65. Duck, S. & Gilmour, R. (Eds.) *Personal Relationships in Disorder* (Personal Relationships 3). Academic Press, London, 1981b.

66. Duck, S. (Ed.) *Repairing Personal Relationships* (Personal Relationships 5). Academic Press, London, 1984.

67. Reid, W. & Shyne, A. *Brief and Extended Casework*. Columbia University Press, New York, 1969.

68. Folkard, M.S., Smith, D. et al. *Impact*. II, HORU Studies, 36, H.M.S.O., London, 1976.

69. Burgess, R. 'Relationships in Marriage and the Family'. In Duck, S. & Gilmour, R. (Eds.) *Studying Personal Relationships* (Personal Relationships 1). Academic Press, London, 1981.

70. Kotler, T. 'A Balanced Distance: Aspects of Marital Quality' *Human Relations*. 38, 5, 1985, 391-408.

71. Moos, R. & Moos, B. 'A Typology of Family Social Environments' *Family Process*. 15, 1976, 357-371.

72. Okell-Jones, C. 'The Family as a Conflict Prone Institution'. In Social Work Services Group, *Violence in the Family: Theory and Practice in Social Work*. H.M.S.O., Edinburgh.

73. Bandler, R. & Grinder, J. *Reframing*. Real People Press, Utah, 1982.

74. Sheldon, B. *Behaviour Modification: Theory, Practice and Philosophy*. Tavistock Publications, London, 1982.

75. Steinglass, P. 'The Roles of Alcohol in Family Systems'. In Orford, J. & Harwin, J. (Eds.) *Alcohol and the Family*. Croom Helm, London, 1982.

76. Minuchin, S. *Families and Family Therapy*. Tavistock Publications, London, 1974.

77. Jenkins, H. 'Orthodoxy in Family Therapy Practice as Servant or Tyrant' *Journal of Family Therapy*. 7, 1985, 19-30.

78. Treacher, A. & Carpenter, J. 'Introduction' *Using Family Therapy*. Blackwell, Oxford, 1984.

79. Ainley, M. 'Family Therapy in Probation Practice'. In Treacher, A. & Carpenter, J. (Eds.) *Using Family Therapy*. Blackwell, Oxford, 1984.

80. Adams, R. & Hill, G. 'The Labours of Hercules: some good reasons why social workers should not try to be different and practise family therapy' *Journal of Family Therapy*. 5, 1, 1983, 71-80.

81. Dimmock, B. & Dungworth, D. 'Creating Manoeuvrability for Family Systems, Systems Therapists in Social Services Departments' *Journal of Family Therapy*. 5, 1983, 53-69.

82. Manor, O. (Ed.) *Family Work in Action: A Handbook for Social Workers*. Tavistock Publications, London, 1984.

83. Ashinger, P. 'Using Social Networks in Counselling' *Journal of Counselling and Development*. 63, 1985, 519-521.

84. Marris, P. *Loss and Change*. Routledge and Kegan Paul, London, 1974.

85. Gorell Barnes, G. *Working with Families*. BASW/Macmillan, London, 1984.

86. Waldrond-Skinner, S. *Developments in Family Therapy*. Routledge and Kegan Paul, London, 1981.

87. Wells, R. 'The Empirical Base of Family Therapy: Practice Implications'. In Tolson, E. & Reid, W. (Eds.) *Models of Family Treatment*. Columbia University Press, New York, 1981.

88. Gurman, A. & Kniskern, D. 'Research on Marital and Family Therapy: Progress, Perspective and Prospect'. In Garfield, L. & Bergin, A. (Eds.) *Handbook of Psychotherapy and Behaviour Change* (2nd edition). Wiley, New York, 1978.

89. Dale, P. et al. *A Systemic View of Child Abuse: Risk, Assessment, Treatment*. Rochdale Child Protection Team, NSPCC, 1982.

90. Reder, P. 'Disorganised Families and the Helping Professions: Who's in charge of what?' *Journal of Family Therapy*. 5, 1, 1983, 23-26.

91. Tolson, E. 'Towards a Meta-model for Eclectic Family Practice'. In Tolson, E. & Reid, W. (Eds.) *Models of Family Treatment*. Columbia University Press, New York, 1981.

92. Segal, L. 'Focussed Problem Resolution'. In Tolson, E. & Reid, W. (Eds.) *Models of Family Treatment*. Columbia University Press, New York, 1981.

93. Carpenter, J. 'Working Together: Supervision, Consultancy and Co-working'. In Treacher, A. & Carpenter, J. (Eds.) *Using Family Therapy*. Blackwell, Oxford, 1984.

94. Wertheim, E. 'Family Unit Therapy and the Science and Typology of Family Systems' *Family Process*. 12, 1973, 361-376.

95. Dale, P. et al. 'A Family Therapy Approach to Child Abuse' *Journal of Family Therapy*. 5, 1983, 117-143.

96. Pinkston, E. et al. 'Parents as Agents for Behaviour Change'. In Schinke, S. (Ed.) *Behavioural Methods in Social Welfare*. Aldine Press, New York, 1981.

97. Hudson, B. *Social Work with Psychiatric Patients*. Macmillan, London, 1982.

98. Scott, R. & Starr, J. 'A Family Oriented 24-Hour Psychiatric and Crisis Service' *Journal of Family Therapy*. 3, 1981, 177-186.

99. Proctor, H. & Stephens, T. 'Family Therapy in the Day Hospital'. In Treacher, A. & Carpenter, J. (Eds.) *Using Family Therapy*. Blackwell, Oxford, 1984.

100. Rack, P. 'Diagnosing Mental Illness: Asians and the Psychiatric Services'. In Khan, V. (Ed.) *Minority Families in Britain*. Macmillan, London, 1979.

101. Hunt, L. *Alcohol Related Problems*. Heinemann, London, 1982.

102. Anderson, S. & Henderson, D. 'Family Therapy in the Treatment of Alcoholism' *Social Work in Health Care*. 8, 4, 1983, 79-84.

103. Cork, R. *The Forgotten Children: A Study of Children with Alcoholic Parents*. Alcoholism and Drug Research Foundation of Ontario, Toronto, 1969.

104. Wilson, C. 'The Impact on Children'. In Orford, J. & Harwin, J. (Eds.) *Alcohol and the Family*. Croom Helm, London, 1982.

105. Parad, H. (Ed.) *Crisis Intervention: Selected Readings*. FSAA, New York, 1965.

106. Rapaport, L. 'Crisis Intervention as a Mode of Brief Treatment'. In Roberts, R. & Nee, R. (Eds.) *Theories of Social Casework*. Chicago University Press, 1970.

107. Hadley, R., Dale, P. & Sills, P. *Decentralising Social Services*. Bedford Square Press, London, 1984.

108. Dryden, J. 'A Social Services Department and the Bengali Community: A New Response'. In Cheetham, J. (Ed.) *Social Work and Ethnicity*. Allen and Unwin, London, 1982.

109. Sandhi, R. 'Ethnicity as a Basis for Problem Solving'. In Cheetham, J. (Ed.) *Social Work and Ethnicity*. Allen and Unwin, London, 1982.

110. Baldock, P. 'Patch Systems: A Change for the Better?' In Sinclair, I. & Thomas, D. (Eds.) *Perspectives on Patch*. NISW Paper 14, London, 1983.

111. Unger, D. & Powell, D. 'Supporting Families under Stress: the Role of Social Networks' *Family Relations*. 29, 4, 1980, 556-574.

112. Bayley, M., Seyd, R., Tennant, A. & Simons, K. 'What Resources Does the Informal Sector Need to Fulfil its Role?' N.I.S.W. Paper 15, The Barclay Report: Papers from a Consultation Day.

113. Smale, G. 'Community Social Work: Synthesis or Compromise?' (unpublished discussion paper).

114. Waters, J. et al. *Family Agency Networks*. Rochdale Child Protection Team, NSPCC, 1984.

115. Speck, R. & Attneave, C. *Family Networks*. Vintage, New York, 1973.

116. Marquis Bishop, S. 'Perspectives on Individual – Family – Social Network Inter-relations' *International Journal of Family Therapy*. 6, 2, 1984, 124-135.

117. Swanson, C. 'Social Networks: Mutual Aid and the Life Model of Practice'. In Germain, C. (Ed.) *Social Work Practice*. Columbia University Press, New York, 1979.

118. Bagarozzi, D. 'The Family Therapist's Role in Treating Families in Rural Communities: A General Systems Approach' *Journal of Marital and Family Therapy*. 8, 2, 1982, 51-57.

119. Challis, D. & Davies, B. 'A New Approach to Community Care for the Elderly' *British Journal of Social Work*. 10, 1980, 1-18.

120. Brake, M. 'Topic Centred Curricula in Social Work Education'. In Bailey, R. & Lee, P. (Eds.) *Theory and Practice in Social Work*. Blackwell, Oxford, 1982.